Dictionary of the Str
English's Most Beaut

MW00929333

A 3500-word lexicon of the most beautiful and interesting words in the English language. This work's aspiration is not a modest one – namely, rescuing from slumbrous, slow-fading oblivion that most beautiful and obscure sliver of the English language – a sliver perhaps too frail and lovely to live were it not for the twitterlight this book may cast upon it. Many entries are obscure words indeed; others less rare yet still beautiful or interesting.

English already has some claim as the best of languages: Italian and French may be more lyrical; German, strident; Turkish, efficient; and Arabic more poetic – yet English is all this and also much more diverse.

May some improve the language further by finding fitting, creative, and colorful usage of these words in our modern, ever-evolving tongue.

– Sir Robin Gizzard Devoe
The Highlands, Alaska – Spring, 2017

"Language is a city to the building of which every human being brought a stone."
– Ralph Waldo Emerson

"Words, like nature, half reveal and half conceal the soul within." – Alfred Lord Tennyson

Notes:
Unusual pronunciations and plurals are noted in
(parentheses).
Etymological information is [bracketed].
Unattributed quotes are original from the
lexagrapher.

Designed by Lazy R Softcovers, Chickaloon, Alaska
Edition Alpha Three – June 2017
ISBN #9781545109274

www.cloudskiing.com

Front cover art: *Seaport with the Embarkation of the
Queen of Sheba* (detail) by French Baroque artist
Claude Lorrain – 1648

Back cover art: *The Course of Empire: Consummation*
(detail) by American Romantic artist Thomas Cole -
1835-36

English's Most Beautiful & Interesting Words

abaft abeam

abask to bask, as in sunshine or genial warmth

abderian given to bouts of laughter
   [after Abdera, in ancient Thrace]

abdominous big-bellied   **abducent** drawing away

abiogenesis theory that living things can generate from
   inanimate matter **abiogenetic**

ablactate wean   **ablepsia** blindness **ableptic**

abnormous irregular; deformed   **aborning** while in the
   process of being born or just beginning

abra a break in a mesa; any narrow mountain pass

abradant an abrading substance

abreact releasing tension; to relieve something, as in a
   repressed emotion, through speaking

abreaction in psychoanalysis, the re-living of an experience in
   order to cathartically purge its emotional dross

abrosia not eating   **absonant** discordant; contrary; against
   a purpose; opposite of consonant

absquatulate to abscond; to decamp; to die

absterge wipe clean; purify; purge

absurdism doctrine that the universe is not rational

abysm an abyss **abysmal abyssal**

abyssopelagic of, similar or pertaining to the ocean depths

accipitral like a hawk or any bird of prey; rapacious

accismus pretending not to be interested in something while
   actually desiring it

acclinate sloping upwards **acclivity** an upward slope

accouchement childbirth

accrescent in botany, growing larger even after flowering

accumbent in botany, (of plants) lying against something

aceldama figuratively, any field or scene of bloodshed

acheronian dismal and dark [from Acheron in Greek
   mythology, the river in Hades that Charon ferried souls of
   the dead across] **acherontic**

acidulous tasting or acting slightly sour; harsh

acock defiantly

acquest something acquired, esp. by force; such an action

acromegalic big-headed   **acronical** occurring at nightfall

acushla term of address; darling [Irish macushla]

addlepated confused; eccentric; flustered

adharma unrighteousness

adhocracy an organizational system designed to be flexible and responsive rather than bureaucratic

adipescent becoming fat or fatty

adjudge to decide; to award   **adminicular** auxiliary

admixture mixing or mingling; something produced by mixing; a mixture; something added while mixing **admix**

adnascent growing on some other thing

adonize to adorn oneself (of men)

adpress to press together

adret the side of a mountain that receives direct sunlight

adsorb to attract and stick to the surface

adultescent an adult whose activities and interests are typically associated with youth culture

adumbral shadowy

adumbrate to outline in a shadowy way, sketch; to vaguely foreshadow; to overshadow   **adunc** hooked

adust (sun)burnt or scorched; dried up by heat; gloomy, sad

advesperate darken; become late

aeneous brass-colored; brassy or golden green colored

aeolian referring or relating to the wind

aeolian harmony harmony or chord progression created from chords of the Aeolian mode – the diatonic scale in common usage in ancient Greek times

aeolist one who pretends to be inspired; a pretentious loquacious bore

aeolistic long-winded   **aeonian** everlasting; lasting for an immeasurably long time period

aerogenic derived from air; gas-producing **aerogenesis**

aerolite or **aerolith** meteorite

aeromancy divination by the state of the air; weather forecasting **aeromantic**

aerugo metal rust; verdigris **aeruginous**

aestival or **estival** of, relating to, or appearing in summer

aestivate or **estivate** to spend the summer, as in a particular manner or at a particular place

aeviternal everlasting, endless

affabulation moral of a fable

affined closely related; connected by an affinity

afflation inspiration

afflatus a sudden rush of poetic or divine inspiration [Latin frattis (to breathe)]

afflux flowing towards or together

afforest to cover with forest; to turn into hunting grounds

affreux frightening **affricate** consonant sound

affusion baptism

afterclap an unexpected damaging or unsettling after-effect or repercussion

aftercome consequence **aftergame** rematch; strategy employed after the first round of action

afterling an inferior **afterpiece** a short comic or dramatic piece performed after a stage play

agape Christian love; love that is spiritual rather than sexual

agelast someone who never laughs

agerasia looking noticeably younger than one actually is

agogic accentuating a musical note by slightly extending its time value

agone ago; past **agrestic** rural; rustic; crude; unpolished

agromania an intense desire to be away from other people or in open spaces

agrypnia sleeplessness **agrypnotic** causing wakefulness

ahimsa in Hinduism & Buddhism, the doctrine of non-violence or the duty of sparing animal life [Sanskrit]

aigrette the egret or the tufted crest and headplumes of an egret; any similarly-shaped feathery excrescences in animals or plants; a spray of feathers or jewels, as in some headdresses **aiguille** a needle-shaped mountain peak

ailuromancy predicting future events (esp. weather) by watching cats' movements **airscrew** aircraft propeller

Aisling an Irish female given name meaning a vision or dream

alabastrine of, pertaining to, or like alabaster

alacrity cheerful promptness

alamort half-dead; dejected or very tired [French a la mort (to the death)] **alate** having wings

alate lately **albicant** or **albescent** white or becoming white

alborado morning song

aleatory dependent on some uncertain contingency or on luck **aleatoric**

alethic of or pertaining to the various modalities of truth, such as the possibility or impossibility of something being true [Greek alētheia (truth)]

alienist therapist **aligerous** winged

aliped wing-footed; having the toes connected by a membrane, serving as a wing, as in bats

allegretto in music, a moderately quick tempo; quicker than andante, not as quick as allegro

allochthonous something originating in a place other than where it is found

allotheism the worship of strange gods

alluvion the flow of water against a shore or bank; flood

allwhither in all directions

alpenstock a stout, adjustable walking stick with a metal point, used by mountain climbers and walkers in hilly or uneven terrain [German]

alpestrine pertaining to the Alps, or other high mountains

alpha rhythm or **alpha wave** a pattern of electrical oscillations in the human brain that occur mostly during wakeful relaxation with closed eyes

altiloquent high-sounding; pompous in speech

altiplano a high plateau or plain, esp. in the Andean regions of Bolivia, Peru, and Argentina **altisonant** high-sounding

altitonant thundering from on high **altivolant** flying high

altricial born helpless and food dependent, said of birds

alveolate deeply pitted, like a honeycomb; honeycombed

alvine of, from, in, or pertaining to, the belly or the intestines

amadelphous living in flocks; gregarious

amain exceedingly; with strength; full-force or full-speed

amaranth an imaginary flower supposed never to fade; purplish red in color

amaranthine undying; immortal; "Where amaranthine gardens gleam." – Clark Ashton Smith

ambsace double aces in card games; bad luck

ambisextrous having both male and females elements; androgenous; bisexual

ambisinister adroit with neither hand (literally, with two left hands) **ambisinistrous**

ambulomancy divination by talking a stroll

ambuscade lying in a wood, concealed, for the purpose of attacking an enemy by surprise; a place in which troops lie hidden, to attack an enemy unexpectedly

amnicolist one who lives near a river

amphigory a nonsense verse that seems to have meaning at first, but proves meaningless

amphiscian relating to or characteristic of someone living in the Tropics

amrita immorality; the ambrosial syrup the drinking of which bestows immortality; ambrosial [Hindu mythology]

anabasis (pl. **anabases**) military expedition

anabatic upward moving, rising

anabiosis a return to life after death or a death-like condition

anabiotic restoring to life

anacampserote a thing that can restore a love thought lost

anacamptic reflecting or reflected sound or light

anaclastic produced by the refraction of light, as seen through water; as, anaclastic curves; refracting; breaking the rectilinear course of light

anacreontic pertaining to or akin to the Greek poet Anacreon; jovial; festive; a short, lyrical poem about love, wine, or both   **anagalactic** beyond our galaxy

anaglypta a thick, embossed wallpaper usually painted over (originally a brand name)

anagogic mystical; interpreting something as having a deeper, spiritual meaning

anagogy an elevation of mind to things celestial; the spiritual meaning or application of words   **analemma** sundial

anamorphic relating to, having, or producing various optically distorted images, as an *anamorphic* lens or perspective

anaphora repetition of the same word(s) at the start of successive clauses, verses or sentences

anaphrodisiac a drug that extinguishes or lessens sexual desire

anastrophe inverting the natural order of words as a rhetorical device

anchorite a hermit; a recluse; one who retires from society into a desert or solitary place, to avoid the temptations of the world and devote himself to religious duties

ancress female anchorite, who withdraws from the world for religious purposes

anechoic free from echoes; sound-absorbent

anemophilous in botany, wind-loving; describing flowering plants that need wind for pollination

anencephalic without a brain

anfractuous full of intricate turns or twists; sinuous

Anima Mundi the vital force, or spiritual essence, of the world [Latin (soul of the world)]   **animastic** spiritual; animate

anoesis in psychology, the mere reception of impressions of sensory or emotional feeling without cognition or understanding

anoetic pertaining to anoesis; unthinkable

anogenic formed from below or beneath

anorectic lacking appetite

anschluss any political union, but originally the one between Germany and Austria in 1938

antejentacular before breakfast   **anteloquy** preface

antelucan before dawn or daylight; esp. applied to the predawn assemblage of early, persecuted Christians

antemundane being or occurring before the creation of the world or before one's birth   **antepast** foretaste

anthelion a halo opposite the sun, consisting of a colored ring or rings around the shadow of the spectator's own head, as projected on a cloud or on an opposite fog bank

anthesis the period or state of full expansion in a flower

antibromic something that destroys offensive smells; a deodorizer

antimacassar ornamented cloth for protecting chair backs

antinovel a fictional work of novel-length, but lacking traditional novelistic elements, such as a straightforward plot structure or realistic characters

antiphrasis the humorous or ironic use of words in a sense opposite to their proper meaning

antipudic intended to cover private parts of the body

antithalian opposed to mirth or festivity   **antre** cavern

apantomancy a form of divination using articles at hand or things that present themselves by chance; apantomancy places special significance on chance meetings of animals [the superstition regarding black cats crossing your path comes from this form of divination]

aperçu a clever insight; an initial view or rapid survey; a summary or outline

aphelion in astronomy, the point in the elliptical orbit of a planet, comet, etc where it is farthest from the sun

aphotic lightless; without sunlight; relating to the depth of a body of water out of sunlight's reach

apian relating to bees   **apical** of or at the apex

apices plural of apex

apiculture raising of bees for their honey and wax

aplomb assurance of manner or of action; self-possession

apocryphal of dubious authenticity; spurious

apolaustic devoted to enjoyment or pleasure-seeking

Apollonian in Greek mythology, resembling the god Apollo; serene; noble; disciplined [opposite of Dionysian]

apotheosis deification

apparatchik member of the Soviet communist bureaucracy; a blindly devoted member of any organization, esp. a large corporation or political party

appersonation in psychiatry, the unconscious belief that one is another person, esp. a famous person

apport the supposed paranormal transference of an object through space, or the appearance of an object seemingly out of nowhere **appose** place near

appulse act of striking against; Astronomy, close approach of two celestial objects or the approach of any planet to a conjunction with the sun, or a star

appurtenance that which belongs to something else; an adjunct; an appendage; an accessory; something annexed to another thing more worthy

apricate to bask in the sun

apricity sunshine; the sun's warmth in winter

aprosexia inability to concentrate

apterous wingless (of insects)

aquarelle a picture made by the application of watercolor through stencils, using a different stencil for each color

aquiferous consisting or conveying water or a watery fluid

araneous transparent; delicate; resembling a cobweb

arbalest type of heavy crossbow

arborescent like a tree, dendritical; branching, tree-shaped

arboricolous growing on or living in trees

arbustum a copse of shrubs or trees; an orchard

Arcadian or **arcadian** ideally rustic or pastoral; peaceful and simple [from ancient Greek region Arcadia]

arcanum (pl. **arcana**) a deep secret; a mystery; a secret essence or elixir

archly in a knowing, clever or mischievous manner; slyly

arcology an extremely large habitat or settlement, sufficient to maintain an internal ecology as well as an extremely high human population density

arctician someone who studies or explores the arctic regions of Earth

arefy to dry or make dry; to wither **argental** of sliver

argenteous silvery **argentocracy** government by money

argentiferous silver-bearing **argle** to argue [British]

argosy a large merchant ship or fleet; a rich supply

argot a secret language or slang peculiar to thieves, vagabonds or any particular group **argotic**

argus one very vigilant; an ever-watchful guardian; a giant in Greek mythology, said to have had a hundred eyes, who was placed by Juno to watch over Zeus's lover Io – after being killed by Hermes, Argus's eyes were transplanted to the peacock's tail [Greek argos (bright)]

argute sagacious; acute; subtle; shrewd

arhat a Buddhist who has achieved enlightenment through rigorous discipline and ascetic practices and at death passes into Nirvana

armisonant resounding with arms or noises of battle

arrhizal in botany, a plant with no roots

arriviste a person who has recently gained power, wealth, success, etc., but not the associated level of respect; upstart; parvenu

arsy-varsy upside-down; wrong end foremost; in a backward or mixed up manner

ashlar a block of hewn stone, esp. dressed for outer placement

ashplant walking stick **asomatous** without a material body; incorporeal

aspergilliform in botany, shaped like a brush

asphodel a plant of southern Europe with clusters of white and yellow flowers; flower in Greek myth said to cover the Elysian Fields

assibilate to pronounce with a hissing, or sibilant, sound

assignation tryst

assonance resemblance of sounds; in poetry, a resemblance in sound or termination, without making rhyme, esp. of the vowel sounds in words; approximate similarity

assuetude accustomedness, habit; habitual use

assurgent ascending; in botany, rising obliquely, curving upward **asthenia** weakness; debility

astraphobia an abnormal fear of thunder and lightning

astrobleme a scar or crater on the earth's surface caused by a meteorite impact

astrogate to navigate in outer space, as a spaceship between stars or planets

ataractic having a tranquilizing effect; a drug that has a tranquilizing effect; "the ataractic halcyons of austral seas"

ataraxia perfect peace of mind, or calmness

atelier a workshop or studio

athanasia or **athanasy** immortality, deathlessness

athymia melancholy; abnormal lack of emotion

atpatruus one's great-grandfather's grandfather's brother

atrabilious inclined to melancholy [Latin atra bilis (black bile)]

atrament blacking; ink **atramentous**

atrous a very black color **attingent** touching

attrahent attracting or drawing; that which attracts, as a magnet **attrist** to sadden

aubade a song or poem concerning or evoking the dawn; a song about lovers parting at dawn

augean filthy **aulic** pertaining to a royal court

aureole a celestial crown added to the bliss of heaven as reward for overcoming matter and the flesh; a halo; in astronomy, the luminescence shining from a celestial body, visible to the unaided eye only during an eclipse

auric of, pertaining to, derived from, or containing gold

aurifex goldsmith **aurulent** gold-colored

auster or **Auster** the south wind **austral**

austringer one who keeps goshawks

autochthonous native; aboriginal; indigenous (opposed to heterochthonous) **autochthonal**

autophanous self-luminous **avast** in seamen's language, cease; stop; stay

avatar the descent of a deity to earth, and his incarnation as a man or an animal; incarnation; manifestation as an object of worship or admiration [Sanskrit]

avaunt away, hence   **aventure** accident; chance; adventure

avernal infernal, chthonic [after Avernus, an Italian lake once reputed (because of its depth and stench) to lead to the underworld; and also believed to kill (with mephetic vapors) birds flying over it] **avernian**

aviatrix a female aviator

avicular of, akin, or pertaining to birds

avizandum in Scottish law, when a judge takes time to privately consider his judgment

avoirdupois excess heaviness or weight of a person

avoy! an expression of surprise

avulse to pluck or pull off by force   **axenic** germ-free

axilla the armpit   **axiomatic** self-evident; aphoristic

azimuth an arc of the horizon intercepted between the meridian of the place and a vertical circle passing through the center of any object; as, the azimuth of a star; the azimuth or bearing of a line surveying

azuline or **azurn** a shade of blue

azure the clear blue color of the sky; the blue vault above; the unclouded sky. "Not like those steps / On heaven's azure" – Milton **azureous azurine**

azured of an azure color; sky-blue. "The azured harebell." –Shakespeare

babeldom a confused sound, perhaps of voices, and resembling that of Babel

bablatrice a female prone to babbling

babushka Russian headscarf

bacchante a female who is a devotee of Bacchus, indulges in drunken revels, or is a noisy drunk **bacchanal**

bacciferous bearing berries

backswept slanted toward the back, as in some hair

baculum a bone or bony structure in the penis of some

mammals (not humans)

baculus rod or staff signifying power or position

baetyl a meteoric stone thought to be of divine origin and worshiped as sacred   **bairn** child

balatron a joker; a clown **balatronic**

baldaquin or **baldachin** a canopy over an altar or throne; a portable canopy borne over shrines in a procession

baldric sword belt

balefire a signal fire; an alarm fire; a funeral pyre

balistarius crossbowman   **balize** a pole raised as a sea beacon or landmark

balneal pertaining to bathing   **balneary** a bathing room

balneation the act of bathing

banausic utilitarian   **bandersnatch** an unfriendly, fictional creature [from the nonsense poem Jabberwocky]

bantling a young or small child; an infant

barathrum a deep pit in Athens, into which condemned criminals were tossed; an abyss; hell; one who is insatiable

barba beard; hair of the human head

barbette a platform within a fortification, which guns were mounted on to fire over the parapet

barbican a tower defending the entrance to a castle or a city

barranca a steep-sided ravine or gorge caused by heavy rains or natural watercourse

bartizan a small, overhanging structure for lookout or defense

bascule an apparatus or structure, such as a drawbridge or seesaw, counterbalanced such that when one end is lowered the other is raised

bathic of or pertaining to depths, esp. of the sea

bathos (BAY-thos) a ridiculous descent from the sublime to the commonplace in writing or speech; an anticlimax, perhaps with humorous effect; sentimentality; mawkishness [Greek bathos (depth)] **bathetic**

bathykolpian deep-bosomed

bathysmal of or pertaining to the depths or bottom of a sea or ocean   **batrachophagous** feeding on frogs

bavardage chattering, prattle; foolish or idle chatter

baxter a baker; originally, a female baker

beatific having the power to impart or complete blissful enjoyment; blissful

beau geste (pl. **beaux gestes**) a gracious gesture, esp. such a gesture that is noble in form or manner, but without substance   **beau monde** the fashionable social scene

beblubber to make swollen and disfigured by weeping   **beblubbered**

beck a small brook; basking in sun or fire   **bedizen** adorn

beeves plural of beef   **beforetime** formerly

bel-esprit a fine genius; a person of great wit

belgard a loving glance

belike likely or probable; perhaps; probably

Bellatrix star in the constellation Orion

bellibone a woman excelling both in beauty and goodness; a fair maid   **bellytimber** food, esp. nutritious food

belliferous bringing war

bellipotent mighty in war; armipotent

belomancy a kind of divination anciently practiced by means of arrows drawn at random from a quiver – occult symbols on the arrows supposedly foretold the future

benedict a newly married man who has long been a bachelor

benignant favorable; kind; gracious   **benison** a blessing

benthic of or pertaining to the bottom of a water body, esp. the ocean; living on the seafloor

benthos flora and fauna living at the bottom of the ocean or other water body

berceuse a lullaby; a tranquil musical composition

bergschrund a crevasse, often large, near a glacier's head

bergwind warm dry wind blowing from a mountainous interior to the coast [Afrikaans]

bersatrix baby-sitter   **besprent** sprinkled, strewed

betide to take place; befall   **betimes** in short time; speedily

bharal blue sheep of Tibet, one of the caprid species

bibliotaph one who hides away books, as in a tomb

biconvex convex on both sides, such as a biconvex lens

bidactyl two-toed   **bierbalk** a church road (such as a path across fields) for funerals

biferous bearing fruit twice a year

bijoutry (pl. **bijoutries**) small articles of jewelry, trinkets, etc.

bildungsroman a novel about the moral, psychological, and spiritual growth of the main (often young) character [German bildung (education) + roman (novel)]

billabong a stagnant pool of water [Australian aboriginal]

billingsgate vituperative or abusive language; profane speech

biloquist one with the ability to speak in two distinct voices

bimanous two-headed   **bimestrial** of two month duration

bioassay or **biological assay** is a scientific experiment conducted to measure the effects of a substance on a living organism

biont any living thing   **bipennate** having two wings

birl to spin   **bisulcate** having two furrows or grooves; cleft or cloven, said of a foot or hoof

blackwork work done by blacksmiths

bladebone the scapula   **blandish** flatter

blandishment words or actions expressing affection or kindness, tending to win the heart or to coax

blatteroon a senseless babbler or boaster

blench to flinch; to quail

blennophobia fear of mucus or slime

blepharal of, like or pertaining to eyelids

bletcherous having an ugly or disgusting design; unaesthetic

bletherskate or **blatherskite** a nonsensical blabberer; an obnoxious braggart   **blink-eyed** habitually winking

blissom to be lustful; to be lascivious; in heat

bloviate to speak at length in a pompous or boastful manner

blunderbuss a short gun or firearm, with a large bore, capable of holding a number of balls, and intended to do execution without exact aim; a stupid, blundering fellow

bodement an omen; portent; prognostic; a fore-showing

bodhi in Buddhism, the state of highest enlightenment

bogglish doubtful; skittish **bolide** a type of bright meteor

bolis a meteor or brilliant shooting star followed by a train of light or sparks, esp. one which explodes

bolson an arid and flat valley surrounded by upland and draining into a central lake

bolus a rounded mass, esp. a soft mass of chewed food

bombilate to hum loudly; to buzz, esp. continuously

boniface an innkeeper **bonnyclabber** coagulated sour milk

bon vivant a jovial companion; one who enjoys the fine things, esp. fine food and drink

booboisie (boob wa ZEE) boobs as a class; the general public regarded as consisting of uncultured or ignorant boobs

boomslang poisonous African tree snake

bootless unavailing; unprofitable; useless

borasco or **borasca** a violent, windy squall oft with a thunderstorm, esp. in the Mediterranean

borborygm or **borborygmus** rumbling of the stomach or intestines caused by gas

boschveldt a plain covered with bush; wilderness [South Africa]

bosh empty talk; contemptible nonsense; an interjection to express disbelief or annoyance **bosket** a grove or thicket

botryoidal having the shape of grapes; grape-like

boulevardier one who frequents the main streets; a worldly and social man

bouleversement a tumult or uproar; a complete overthrow; a turning upside down

bounder a cad; an ill-mannered, loud, or unscrupulous person; one who limits **bourasque** a tempest or storm

brachiation movement by swinging arms from one hold to the next, as through trees

bracken a widespread, weedy fern; an area an area overgrown with such ferns

brain wave sudden inspiration **brainsick** mad

brancard cot, litter **brank** to prance; to caper; to toss the head, as a horse trying to spurn the bit

brannigan a drinking spree

breastsummer a summer or girder extending across a building flush with, and supporting, the upper part of a front or external wall

breedbate one who breeds or originates quarrels

breloque a charm or small piece of jewelry, often attached to a watch chain

breviloquence a brief and pertinent mode of speaking **breviloquent**

bricolage the haphazard effect of proximate buildings having been constructed in different styles or different historical time periods; construction using materials at hand

brickbat a piece of broken brick, esp. one used to throw at someone or something; any rock-like missile used in a such a way; an inflammatory or caustic criticism

bridewell a jail; a house of correction for disorderly persons [after a 1553 hospital built near St. Bride's Well in London]

brigadoon an idyllic place that is unrealistic, or unaffected by time; a place that makes its appearance for a brief period in a long time [from Brigadoon, a village in the musical Brigadoon, that is under a spell wherein it is invisible to outsiders except on one day every 100 years]

brigandine or **brigantine** Middles Ages coat of armor, consisting of metal scales sewed to linen

brightwork polished metal parts, esp. on ships or vehicles

brigue to intrigue

brindled having dark streaks or spots, as a brindled lion

brisance the violence of an explosion, explosiveness; the destructive effect of the energy from an explosion; volatility, high likelihood of explosion [perhaps from Latin brisa (post-crushed grape refuse) or Irish brissim (I break)]

brocket deer   **broma** food; aliment

bromide a tired remark; a platitude; a dull or boring person

bromidic corny; trite   **bromidrosis** foul-smelling perspiration [Greek bromos (stench)]

bronteum in ancient theater, a device used to imitate the sound of thunder

brontide a sound like distant thunder caused by seismic effects; sound of distant thunder

brontophobia fear of thunder storms; fear of thunder or lightning   **brown study** very deeply absorbed in thought or inner reflection

brume fog, mist, or vapors   **brumous** foggy; misty

buccula a double chin; fold of fat under the chin

bucolic pastoral; rustic; of or pertaining to the life of a shepherd   **bumfuzzle** to confuse or bewilder

burble gushy speech; to babble rapidly; a bubbling sound

burke to dispose of quietly or indirectly; to suppress; to smother; to shelve, as to burke a parliamentary question

buss a kiss; a rude or playful kiss

buttling past participle of buttle; acting as a butler

buzzwig a large bushy wig; an important person

Byronic like one who is melancholic, passionate, melodramatic, and disregards societal norms

byssine made of silk; having a silky or flax-like appearance; having many threads

cabalism a superstitious devotion to the mysteries of the religion which one professes

cabotinage overacting; hamming

cabotage shipping and sailing between points in the same country; trade or navigation in coastal waters

cachalot sperm whale

cachet a symbolic mark of distinction or authenticity; stamp of approval; a seal on a document

cacodemon an evil spirit or a demon   **cacodaemonic**

cacoethes compulsion; mania

cacogen a person of antisocial bent
   [Greek kakogenes (of lowly birth)]

cacography incorrect or bad handwriting or spelling

cacotopia a place where everything is as bad as it can be, esp. government [opposite of utopia]

caesura a natural pause in a line of verse; pause or interruption in conversation **caesural**

cafard sadness; depression; melancholy **caftan** a cloak extending down to the ankle

calamist one who plays upon a reed or pipe

calamistrate to curl or fizz, as the hair

calamus a rush or reed used anciently as a pen to write on parchment or papyrus; the horny basal portion of a feather

calescent increasing in warmth; growing warm or hot

caliginous dim; obscure; dark; gloomy; misty

calix (pl. **calices**) cup; chalice **callant** a boy; a lad

callipygian possessive of a nicely shaped arse **callipygous**

callithump a mildly riotous parade, esp. with tin horns blowing or other discordant noises

callomania delusions that oneself is extremely beautiful; having inordinate love of beauty **calvous** bald

calyx (pl. **calyces)** the outer covering of a flower

camarilla the private audience chamber of a king; a company of secret and irresponsible advisers, as of a king; a cabal or clique **camelry** troops mounted on camels

camerated in architecture, arched, vaulted; in zoology, divided into separate chambers

camisade or **camisado** a surprise attack by night or at break of day, when the enemy was presumed to be abed

campestral of, like or pertaining to the countryside; of, relating to, or growing in open fields

canaille the lowest class of people; the vulgar; the proletariat; rabble; riffraff

canard a false (esp. malicious) report, fabricated and spread as by a newspaper; a hoax

candent heated to whiteness; glowing with heat

candescent glowing hot; white-hot; luminous; incandescent

canescent hoary; growing white or gray; assuming a color approaching to white

canicular of or relating to Sirius, the Dog Star; pertaining to the "dog days" of summer

cannonarchy government by superior military force, or by cannons

canopus ancient Egyptian vase for holding the inner organs of the dead

canorous melodious; musical; singing; resonant

cant the idioms and peculiarities of speech in any sect, class, or occupation; language peculiar to a certain group

cantabank a strolling singer; a common or second-rate singer or musician

cantabile in a melodious, flowing style, esp. in music

cantatrice female singer

canterbury a type of stand that includes divisions for holding books or music

canticle song; chant; a sung prayer or short holy song

cantillate to chant or intone

cantle corner, edge, slice or part of something; a piece cut out of something

caparison ornamental covering for a horse; the harness or trappings of a horse, taken collectively, esp. when decorative; richly ornamented clothing; finery

capernoited capricious; slightly feeling the effects of alcohol

capillaceous having long filaments; resembling a hair; slender

capistrate hooded; cowled

capnomancy divination by watching smoke

capreolate in botany, having tendrils, or filiform spiral claspers, by which plants fasten themselves to other bodies; having or resembling tentacles

capric having a goat-like or sweaty smell; of, like or pertaining to goats   **caprid** of or pertaining to the ruminants which include goats, or the genus Capra

capriform goat-like   **caprine** of, like or pertaining to goats

capriole a straight up leap that a horse makes with all fours, with a kick of the hind legs when at the leap's apex; a leap or caper, as in dancing

carapace the thick shell of turtle, crab, and other crustaceans

carnassial adapted for eating flesh

carneous fleshy; having the qualities of flesh; flesh-colored

carnifex an executioner or hangman

carnification the act or process of turning to flesh

carnificial pertaining to or belonging to an executioner or a butcher

Cartesian of or relating to Descartes, his theories, methods, or philosophy, esp. its emphasis on mechanistic interpretation [from Cartesius, Latin form of Descartes, after René Descartes]

Carthaginian Peace any draconian peace treaty with very harsh terms

cartouche in architecture, an ornamental figure, esp. on an oval shield; in Egyptian hieroglyphics, an oval figure containing characters that represent the names of royal or divine people; a paper cartridge; a wooden case filled with balls, to be shot from a cannon; a gunner's bag for ammunition; a military pass for a soldier on leave

carucate the area of land a team of oxen can plow in one season – about 100 acres

casemate a chamber intended to be bombproof in which cannon may be placed or troops housed

Cassandra one whose prophesies are unheeded [after Cassandra in Greek mythology who received the gift of prophecy but was cursed by Apollo never to be believed]

castellum a small, isolated fortress of the ancient Romans

castral of, characteristic of, or pertaining to a camp

castrametation the art or act of encamping; the making or laying out of a camp

catachthonian or **catachthonic** subterranean; underground

catacoustics or **cataphonics** branch of the science of acoustics that covers echoes or reflected sounds

cataglottism kissing using the tongue, French kissing

catamount(ain) wild cat; cougar

cataphasia speech disorder in which one repeats a word or phrase several times, or constantly

cataphysical unnatural; perverse; contrary to natural or evolutionary laws

catastasis that part of drama play just before the climax

catawampus or **cattywampus** askew; crooked; not properly lined up; out of whack; a fierce imaginary creature said to inhabit forests; diagonally positioned, catercornered

catbird seat a position of power, prominence, or advantage

catchpenny something worthless, particularly a book or pamphlet, adapted to the popular taste, and intended to bilk money from the ignorant or unwary

catenate to connect in a series of links, as in or by a chain

cathect to inject with libidinal, emotional or mental energy

cathedra the official chair or throne of a bishop, or of any person in high authority **cathedratic**

cathexis in psychoanalysis, the concentration of libido or emotional energy on a single object or idea, or activity; obsession **catholicon** cure-all; panacea

catogenic formed from above

catoptric of, relating to, or produced by mirrors or reflections

catoptromancy divination by a sick person looking at their reflection in a mirror submerged in water – a distorted image boded ill, a healthy looking image was favorable

cavernicolous living in caves **celadon** pale green

celandine a species of yellow-flowered plant, oft growing on old walls or among garbage

celation concealment; concealing a pregnancy **celative**

celsitude loftiness; height; elevation **cembalo** harpsichord

cenacle small dining room

cenatory of, like or pertaining to supper

cenotaph a tomb or a monument in honor of a person (or a group) whose remains are elsewhere [Greek kenotaphion, from kenos (empty) + taphos (tomb)]

cenote deep natural well, esp. in the limestone of the Yucatan

centesimal a hundredth part; relating to or divided into hundredths **cephalic** pertaining to the head

cephalopod any mollusc, of the class Cephalopoda, which includes squid, cuttlefish, octopus, etc., often having tentacles attached to a large head

ceraceous resembling wax

ceraunomancy divination by using thunderbolts [Greek ceraunos (thunderbolt)]

cerberic vigilant; dragon-like; like Cerberus [3-headed dog guarding Hades in Greek myth]

cerebration mental action of the brain, both conscious and unconscious; thinking carefully

cerebrotonic designating or resembling a type of personality which is introverted, intellectual, shy, and emotionally restrained

cerecloths or **cerements** cloths dipped in wax and used as burial garments

Ceres in Roman mythology, the goddess of agriculture and corn; the largest asteroid in our solar system

cerise a vivid purplish red; color of ripe cherries; a light, bright red

cernuous in botany, inclining or nodding downward; pendulous; drooping

cerulescent close to cerulean, or sky blue **cerulean**

cerulific producing a blue or sky color **cerumen** earwax

cetaceous of or relating to whales or to any marine mammal of the order Cetacea

chameleonic resembling a chameleon; readily changing color or other attributes

champaign flat, open country; "Through Alpine vale or champaign wide" – Wordsworth

chantage blackmail; extorting money by threatening to expose scandalous facts

chantefable in medieval French literature, a story written in prose and verse

chanteuse a female singer, esp. a nightclub singer

chantepleure singing and crying that is simultaneous or alternates; a small hole in a wall designed to let water pass

chaogenous (kay OJ en us) that which originates from chaos, or is chaos-born

charientism a gracefully-veiled insult; taunting language softened by jocularity

charnel containing dead bodies; a graveyard; deathlike; sepulchral **chartaceous** papery **chartless** unmapped

chasmophile someone who loves nooks and crannies

chatelaine the mistress of a castle or large household; a clasp worn at the waist with handkerchief, keys, etc.

chatoyant having a varying luster, or color, like that of a cat's eye by night [French chatoyer (to shine like a cat's eye)]

chatter marks indents in wood left by errant hammer strokes

cheiloproclitic having an attraction to a person's lips

chela a grasping claw, such as on a lobster or scorpion

chelonian of, like or pertaining to tortoises or turtles

chersonese peninsula **chesil** gravel

chevalier a horseman or knight; a gallant young man

chevaline horseflesh

chevelure a head of hair; a periwig; the coma or nebulous section of a comet

chiasmus inversion of the second of two parallel clauses

chignon a knot or mass of real or fake hair worn at the back of the head or nape

chiliad a group of 1,000; millennium

chiliahedron a figure of one-thousand sides

chiliarch military commander of a thousand men in Hellenistic Greece **chiliastic** millenarian

chiliomb sacrifice of one thousand oxen (or other animals)

chimera fanciful scheme; illusion; an organism having genetically different tissues [after Chimera, a fire-breathing female monster in Greek mythology who had a lion's head, a goat's body, and a serpent's tail – from Greek khimaira (she-goat)]

chiminage a toll for passage through a forest

chinoiserie (shin-wahz-ree) anything reflecting Chinese culture, esp. Chinese style in art; Chinese artifacts or knickknacks; Chinese manner of doing things

chirk to enliven; to make or become cheerful; lively;

in good spirits

chirm collective term for goldfinches; noise; din; esp. confused noise, clamor, or hum of many voices, notes of birds, etc.; to chirp or to make a mournful cry, as a bird

chirography (ky-ROG-ruh-fee) the art of writing with one's own hand; art of telling fortunes by examining hands

chiropteran a bat; a mammal of the order Chiroptera, with forelimbs serving as modified wings

chirotonsor a barber

chiton an under garment among the ancient Greeks, nearly representing the modern shirt

chocolate-box having a romanticized beautiful image; stereotypically or superficially pretty [from pictures sometimes seen on boxes of chocolate]

chrematophobia fear of money

christie or **christy** a ski turn performed by shifting weight forward and turning with skis parallel

chromogenic producing color

chromosphere in astronomy, the faint pink extension of a star's atmospheric envelope between the corona and the photosphere

chryselephantine composed of, or adorned with, gold and ivory

chrysopoetics transmutation of something into gold

chthonian subterranean; pertaining to the underworld; living beneath the earth

chthonic (THON-ik) of or relating to the earth or the underworld; living under the earth; dark, primitive and mysterious

chunter or **chunner** to complain vocally, esp. in a constant, low, often incomprehensible manner; to grumble

cicatrix a scar

cilium (pl **cilia**) an eyelash; a microscopic hairlike appendage extending from the surface of an organism; in botany, one of the hairs along the edge of a leaf or other structure

cimelia a collection of treasures in a royal or church treasury

cimmerian dark and gloomy [from Cimmerians in Homer's Odyssey: a people who lived in a land of everlasting night]

cinereous like or consisting of ashes

cingular of or pertaining to a cingulum, a band or girdling part of an animal or plant; encircling, girdling, surrounding [Latin cingulum (girdle): also the root in cincture, precinct, and succinct]

cingulomania a strong desire to hold someone in your arms

cinnabar a deep red mineral, mercuric sulfide; a bright red color tinted with orange

circean like Circe; pleasing or enchanting, but also depraving or debasing [from Circe in the Odyssey who first charmed Odysseus's men, and then turned them into animals]

circumambient surrounding; encompassing; inclosing or being on all sides; esp. used of the air about the earth

circumaviate to fly around

circumbendibus circumlocution; an indirect manner of traveling, speaking, or writing

circumcrescent growing around, above, or over

circumfloribus flowery and long-winded

circumforaneous going about; wandering from place to place, as a circumforaneous musician

circumfulgent shining around

circumfuse to pour around; to surround (with a fluid); suffuse

circumgyration the act of turning, rolling, or whirling round

circumjacent bordering on every side; surrounding

circumlittoral around or near the shore

circumpose to place around

circumspect attentive to all the circumstances of a case or the probable consequences of an action; cautious; prudent

circumvallate to surround with a rampart or wall

circumvest to cover round, as with a garment

circumvolant flying around

circumvolute to twist around; to encircle; to enwrap

circumvolution something sinuous   **circumvolve** to revolve

cisalpine on the hither side of the Alps with reference to

Rome; on the south side of the Alps

cislunar situated between the earth and the moon

cismarine on the near side (or this side) of the ocean

cismontane this side of the mountains

cispontine on this or the near side of the bridge

cisvestism wearing clothing that is strange or not appropriate

civitas a body of people comprising an organized community

clapperclaw to claw with fingernails; to use abusive language towards; to scold harshly; to cruelly toy with

clapter clapping or clap-like sound; applause, esp. from a large crowd

claque persons hired to applaud at a performance; a group of adoring admirers   **claudication** lameness; a limping

claustral of or like a place of religious seclusion

claver chatter

clavilux coined by the artist Thomas Wilfred, a mechanical device used to create and perform Lumia, WIlfred's term for Light Art [Latin (light played by key)]

cleave to split, divide, or rive (past participle **cloven**, **cleft** or **cleaved**); to cling, to adhere; to make or accomplish by or as if by cutting; to pierce or penetrate; to make one's way

clepsydra ancient device that used the flow of water to measure time

cleptobiosis when one species, such as of ants, steals food from another

clerisy intelligentsia; scholars and educated people as a class

clinkstone type of igneous rock that makes a ringing sound when struck

clinquant glittering, esp. with gold or tinsel; tinsel; glitter

clishmaclaver gossip   **clithridiate** key-hole-shaped

clitter to make a piercing rattling sound   **clivose** hilly; steep

cloaca a waste pipe for sewage or surface water; sewer; toilet; cesspool of moral filth

cloacal pertaining to sewers; concerned with or full of obscenity or indecency   **clochard** a tramp or vagrant

clock-star a star whose movement is used to regulate

timepieces   **cloisonne** artistic design

clotheshorse a frame used to hang dry clothes; a person obsessed with dress

cloud-built fanciful; imaginary; chimerical; fantastic

cloud-cuckoo-land or **cloud cuckoo land** an idealized, unrealistic state or place

clough ravine; trench; gully   **clowder** collective term for cats

clumperton a clownish and clumsy lout

clusterfist a clownish boor; a tightwad

coaming the raised edge around ship's hatches, designed to keep out water

cochlear spiral-shaped; twisted spirally

cockalorum an egoist; boastful talk

cockatrice a serpent hatched from a cock's egg and having the power to kill by its glance

cockloft small room just under the roof

cockshut evening; twilight

coda the concluding passage of a piece of music, added to give a satisfactory conclusion; additional section at the end of a piece of literature; any concluding part

codswallop something utterly senseless; nonsense; balderdash

coffle animals or people chained together in a line, esp. slaves so chained; "the stench of your coffled chattel o'erwhelms all civilized sense"

cogitabund meditative; engaged in deep thought

cognoscente (pl. **cognoscenti**) person with specialized knowledge or highly refined taste; a connoisseur

collachrymate to weep together; to commiserate

collachrymation a collective weeping

collapsar black hole   **collectanea** collected writings

colligate connect logically

colliquate to melt; to dissolve; to change from solid to fluid; to become liquid

collogue (kuh-LOG) to talk or confer secretly and confidentially; to converse, esp. with evil intentions;

to plot mischief   **colloid** gelatinous

collop a slice of meat or fold of flab

colluvium rock fragments, sand, etc. accumulated at the foot of a slope or cliff

collywobbles butterflies in the stomach; bellyache

colorable plausible

coltish lacking discipline; lively and playful

colubrine of or like a snake

commove disturb   **complect** to embrace; to interweave

comport to conduct or behave (oneself) in a particular manner; to agree or harmonize; to suit

compossible possible in coexistence with something else; compatible

compotator a drinking companion   **conation** impulse

concatenate to link together; to unite in a series or chain, as things depending on one another

concinnous suitable; pleasant; elegant; neatly arranged, without loose ends   **concinnity**

concrescent growing together

condign well-deserved, appropriate

confabulate to talk familiarly together; to chat; to prattle; in psychology, to unconsciously misremember fact as fantasy

conflate to fuse, combine, or blend; to confuse

conflation a fusing together; merger of two or more things or ideas into one   **conflux** a confluence

confrere a colleague or fellow, esp. a professional one

congeries a collection of things into one mass; a heap

consanguine or **consanguineous** akin; related by blood

consonance agreement; accord; congruity; harmony

conspectus a general sketch or outline of a subject

constellate to combine as a cluster; to unite as in a constellation

constringe tighten   **consuetude** custom, habit, familiarity

contect to cover or overlay

conterminous having the same bounds, or limits; bordering upon; contiguous; coextensive; having the same scope, range of meaning, or temporal extent

contesseration harmonious union

contretemps an unexpected and untoward accident; something inopportune or embarrassing

contrist to sadden   **contubernal** living together, esp. in the same tent; cohabiting in any manner

conurbation a mostly urban region, including dense urban cores, adjacent towns and suburbs

convolve to roll or wind together; to roll or twist one part on another

convoke to call together; to assemble by summons; convene

coparceny an equal share of an inheritance

coprolite fossilized excrement

coprophagan a kind of beetle that feeds on dung

coprophagous feeding on excrement

coprophilia having great interest in feces

coprostasis constipation; costiveness

copse thicket of small trees or shrubs; coppice

coquelicot a wild poppy; brilliant red; poppy red; orange-scarlet color

coquillage shell-like decoration

coracle a small, oblong boat made of wickerwork and waterproofed with hides or pitch, able to be piloted and carried by one person

corbeau blackish green; very dark green

corium dermis; a sub-layer of skin

corm in botany, a bulbous subterranean part of a stem

cornelian or **carnelian** a hard reddish-brown form of quartz

corniche a coastal road, esp. one cut into a cliff; a seaside promenade

cornucopian pertaining to the horn of plenty; creating a never ending supply; overflowing with food, fruit, etc.

cornuted cuckolded   **cornuto** cuckolder

coronach funeral dirge

corrade erode   **corrivate** to cause to flow together

coruscant glittering or flashing

coruscate to glitter or sparkle in flashes; to flash; to exhibit dazzling virtuosity

corybantic wildly excited; frenzied; madly agitated

cosmocrat or **kosmokrator** ruler or prince of the world; a prosperous business man living a global lifestyle

cosmogony the study of the creation of the world or universe; a particular theory or mythology of such creation **cosmogonic**

cosmographic relating to the general description of the universe **cosmolatry** worship of the world

cosmoplastic pertaining to the formation of the world, esp. independently of God; world-forming

cosmopoietic creating the universe

cosmopolis city whose inhabitants are from diverse countries

cosmotheism the belief that equates God with the cosmos; pantheism **costellate** ribbed

costive slow to act or to speak; sluggish; constipated

coteau an upland; moderately high region of ground

coterie a circle of people who associate with one another; an exclusive group of people, who associate closely for a common purpose; a clique

cothurnal of, like or pertaining to drama or tragedy

counterblast a work that strongly criticizes, defies, or refutes another; a defiant denunciation

counterfoil part of a check that is kept by the check writer

counterphobic seeking out something that is feared, esp. to overcome that fear

counterpoise to act against with equal weight; to equal in weight; to counterbalance

countersign a secret signal, word or phrase, esp. given to guards with orders to let none pass without knowing the sign; a password; a secret sign given in answer to another

countervail to act against with equal force; to counterbalance or compensate

coxcomb a vain, showy fellow; a conceited, silly man, fond of display

coxcomical vain; conceited; silly; of or like a coxcomb

cozenage fraud; artifice **crackjaw** difficult to pronounce; such a word or phrase

crankle to break into bends, turns, or angles; to crinkle

crapulent or **crapulous** suffering from or prone to overeating or drinking **crapulence**

craquelure fine cracking on old paintings

crebrous frequent, numerous

credenda in theology, things to be believed; articles of faith (distinguished from agenda, or practical duties)

cremnophobia fear of precipices and cliffs

Cremona a fine violin made in Cremona, Italy by either the Amati family or by Stradivarius

crenelated or **crenellated** having battlements, or repeated square indentations like a battlement

crepitate to crackle; to snap

crepitus the noise produced by a sudden discharge of wind from the bowels **crepuscle** or **crepuscule** twilight

crepuscular like or pertaining to twilight; glimmering "crepuscular depths of personality" – William James [Latin crepusculum (twilight)]

crescive growing; increasing

crestfallen dispirited; dejected; cowed

cri de coeur an impassioned outcry (as of appeal or protest) [French (cry from the heart)]

cribble to pass something through a sieve; to sift

cribration sifting

cribellum (pl. **cribella**) an organ with many fine pores, used for spinning silk in some spiders

crinal of or pertaining to the hair

crispate (botany) having curled, wavy or notched edges

crolulent suitable, apt, acceptable, excellent

cromlech prehistoric monument of monoliths placed around a mound; a dolmen

croodle to cower or cuddle together, as from fear or cold; to coo, as a dove

crossbuck x-shaped sign at a railroad intersection

cruciferous bearing a cross

crwth or **crowth** or **crowd** an ancient, violin-like, six-stringed musical instrument of Celtic origin

cryptadia a grouping of things that are to be kept hidden

cryptaesthetic of, like or pertaining to extrasensory perception **cryptesthesia**

cryptoclastic composed of rock fragments too small to see with the naked eye

cryptogenic of uncertain or unknown origin

cryptomnesia the phenomenon of the reappearance of a long-forgotten memory as if it were a new experience

cryptonym a secret name; a name by which a person is known only to the initiated

cryptozoology study of animals whose existence is unproven

cuckquean a woman who has an unfaithful husband

cucullate hooded; cowled; covered as with a hood; hood-shaped

cuesta (KWEST-ah) a hill or ridge with a steep face or cliff on one side and a gentler slope on the other [Spanish costa (side, rib)]

culex the genus that includes gnats and mosquitoes

culmen top; summit; acme

cumberground a person or thing that just takes up space

cumbrous cumbersome

cumshaw a tip for service; baksheesh

cupric of, pertaining to, or derived from, copper; containing copper

curglaff the shock of suddenly jumping into cold water [Scottish]

curple buttocks; rump   **curtilage** in law, a yard, courtyard, or piece of ground attached to a dwelling

curvet to leap; to frisk; to frolic

curvilinear or **curvilineal** in geometry or art, formed by curved lines; having bends; curved

cutpurse one who cuts purses for the sake of stealing them or their contents (an act common when men wore purses fastened by a string to their girdles); a pickpocket

cwm a steep, glacially-formed valley roughly shaped like an amphitheater; a cirque

cwtch a hiding place; a cubbyhole; to cuddle or hug [Welsh]

cyaneous sky blue; cerulean; azure

cyanometer instrument for measuring degrees of blueness, esp. of the sky or ocean

cybernate to control by means of a computer, esp. an industrial process

cyclothymia mild form of bipolar disorder, or manic-depressive psychosis **cyclothymic**

cygnet a young swan

cymric (KIM ric) of, relating to, or like the non-Gaelic Celtic people of Britain or their language [Welsh cymru (Welsh)]

cytherean pertaining to the goddesses Aphrodite or Venus, thus also pertaining to beauty

cytheromania nymphomania

czarevna proper title of an imperial Russian czar's daughter

dactylogram a fingerprint

daedal having an ingenious or complex design; finely or skillfully created; artistic **daedalian**

daeva a supernatural entity with a disagreeable nature [Avestan language (a being of shining light)]

damascene of or relating to Damascus

damask linen woven with a pattern produced by the different directions of the thread, without contrast of color; Damascus steel or the wavy pattern of such steel; a deep pink or rose color

damson a very deep purple color; color of damson tree fruit

dapatical sumptuous; expensive

Daphnean shy and beautiful

darbies handcuffs **darkle** to grow or make dark

darshan an audience with a spiritual leader; euphoria, grace or blessedness derived from same

daven to pray, esp. to recite the Jewish liturgy **davening**

daymare a terrifying experience, similar to a nightmare, felt while awake

deasil clockwise, or in the same direction the sun moves

debark to disembark

debouch to march out from a confined place into an open area; to emerge or issue from a narrow area into the open

debride to remove necrotic tissue from a wound

decarnate divested of bodily or physical form

declivity a steep slope   **declivitous** steeply sloped

decimestrial lasting or containing ten months

decollate to behead   **decollation** beheading

decrassify to make less crass; to clean of dirt

decrescent decreasing; becoming less by gradual diminution; as a decrescent moon   **decrescence**

decuman very large; a large wave

decumbent lying down; recumbent

decumbiture confinement to bed by an invalid, or the time so spent

decurrent extending downward

defervescence a fever's abatement

deflagrate to set fire to, esp. all of a sudden

deflexure a bending down; a turning aside; deviation

defluent running or flowing down; decurrent

defter notebook

degringolade a rapid decline or sudden deterioration

degust to taste and fully appreciate; to relish or savor

dehisce to open by dehiscence, as the bursting of plant pod; to gape

deinotherian quite large; elephantine [from Deinotherium, a genus of prehistoric elephant-like mammals]

deiparous bearing or bringing forth a god

dejecta feces; excrement   **delassation** fatigue

delectation delight; enjoyment; great pleasure

delenda things to be erased or blotted out

delibate to taste; to take a sip of; to dabble in

deliquesce to melt away or to appear to melt into nothing; in chemistry, to dissolve gradually and become liquid by attracting and absorbing moisture from the air, as certain salts and acids **deliquescent**

deliquium a swooning or fainting; liquefaction through absorption of moisture from the air; a lazy, maudlin mood; a blocking of the sun's light, from an eclipse or other cause

deliriant tending to produce delirium; hat which induces a medical state of frank delirium, esp. in reference to a drug

delirium tremens a violent delirium induced by withdrawal after prolonged alcohol abuse

delitescent lying hid; concealed

delphian prophetic, oracular

delphically prophetically; obscurely

Delphic of or relating to Delphi, or to the famous oracle of that place; (often lowercase) ambiguous; mysterious; oracular; prophetic; brotherly

demagogue a leader of the rabble; one who attempts to control the multitude by specious or deceitful arts; an unprincipled and factious mob orator or political leader

démarche a decisive or well-finessed diplomatic action, esp. one starting a new policy

demersal sinking to the bottom of the sea; subaqueous; living underwater or near the sea bad

demilune crescent, half-moon; crescent-shaped

demimonde a class of women kept by wealthy lovers or protectors; women prostitutes considered as a group; mistress [French, literally: half-world]

demisang halfbreed

demiurge God, as maker of the world; something that is an autonomous creative force

demulcent softening; mollifying; soothing; assuasive

demur to take exception

dendrophilous loving trees; characterized by an arboreal way of life   **dentagra** toothache

deportment manner of deporting one's self; manner of acting; conduct; carriage; esp. manner of acting with respect to the courtesies and duties of life; demeanor

depredate to plunder; to lay waste; to prey upon

dermis the deep sensitive layer of the skin beneath the scarfskin or epidermis; also called true skin, derm, derma, corium, cutis, and enderon

descensive tending to descend; tending downwards; descending   **descrive** to describe

desideratum (pl. **desiderata**) that which is desired; any improvement which is wanted

desiderium a fervent desire, esp. for something formerly possessed and now missed; emotional pain from missing something or someone

despumate to throw off impurities in spume; to work off in foam or scum; to foam   **desudation** profuse sweating

desuetude the cessation of use; disuse; inactivity

desultory jumping from one thing or subject to another, without order or rational connection; without logical sequence; disconnected

detenebrate to remove darkness from; to free from obscurity

deturpate to defile or disfigure

devenustate to deprive of beauty or grace; to disfigure

devil theory the theory of history that political and social crises are caused by the deliberate actions of evil or ill-informed leaders rather than being the natural result of conditions

dewclaw a small claw on the feet of some animals that doesn't reach the ground

diablerie sorcery; deviltry; mischief; having dealings with demons or devils   **diabrotic** corrosive

diaglyph sunken engraving on a stone or gem; intaglio

diamagnetic any substance, as bismuth or glass that, unlike iron, tends to take a position at right angles to the lines of magnetic force, and is repelled by either pole of a magnet

diamantiferous yielding diamonds

diamantine like or consisting of diamonds

dianoetic pertaining to thought or to the discursive faculty

diapason concord, as of notes an octave apart; harmony; a full expression of harmonious sound; an instrument's or a voice's entire range

diaphanous translucent or transparent; pellucid; clear; of such fine texture as to allow the passage of light; having a delicacy of form; vague or insubstantial

diaphoretic having the power to increase perspiration; sudorific; sweating   **dicephalous** two-headed

didder to totter, as a child in walking; to move in a trembling fashion

dido a shrewd trick; an antic; a caper; a prank

diestrus or **dioestrus** a state or interval of sexual inactivity or quiescence between periods of activity – of mammals having several estrous cycles in one breeding season

diffinity completely dissimilar or lacking in affinity

digerati collectively, people who are considered the elite (for whatever reason) in information technology [digital + literati]

digladiate to fight like gladiators; to contend fiercely; to dispute violently   **digladiation**

dilacerate to tear; to rend asunder; to separate by force

dilaniate to rend in pieces; to tear

diluent something used to dilute

diluvial of or pertaining to a flood or deluge, esp. to the great deluge in the days of Noah; diluvian; in geology, effected or produced by a flood or deluge of water

diluvium a flood; something deposited by a flood

dimidiate divided into two equal parts; reduced to half in shape or form

dimorphous or **dimorphic** existing in two distinct forms

dingle, dimble or **dumble** a narrow dale; a small dell; a small, secluded, and embowered valley

dinic pertaining to dizziness

dionysian uninhibited; spontaneous; wild; orgiastic [from Dionysus, the god of wine and fertility in Greek mythology]

diogenic cynical   **dioptric** transparent; assisting vision by means of the refraction of light; refractive

dioptrics the branch of optics concerned with refraction

dirigisme any economy where the government exerts a strong directive influence, often with many but not all of the characteristics of a centrally-planned economy

dirigiste controlled or guided by a central authority, as in an economy

disabuse to free a person from believing a falsehood or an error

disafforest to clear of trees; to deforest

disbosom to express pent-up feelings (to someone); to make known; to reveal; to unbosom

discalced barefoot; unshod   **discerp** tear to pieces; to rend; to tear off

discommode to trouble   **discommodious** inconvenient

discountenance to refuse to support; to discourage

discursive passing from one thing to another; ranging over a wide field; roving; digressive; desultory

dishabille extreme casual or disorderly dress; very casual attire; a purposefully careless manner

dishallow to make unholy, to profane

dispiteous having no pity; cruel; furious

disposophobia compulsive hoarding; the fear of disposing of anything

displuviate in some way protected from rain

disprize to undervalue or scorn

distal remote from the point of attachment or origin, as the distal end of a bone or muscle

dithyrambic pertaining to or resembling a dithyramb [in ancient Greek poetry, a hymn in honor of Bacchus, full of transport and poetical rage]; wild and boisterous; very enthusiastic; wild and emotional speech or writing

diurnation the condition of sleeping or becoming dormant by day

divagate to wander about or meander; to stray from a

subject, focus, or course

dizen to dress gaudily; to overdress; to bedizen

dizzard a fool or idiot

dogmatic stubbornly opinionated; arrogant; overbearing in asserting and maintaining opinions; relying upon dogma or settled opinion, as opposed to empirical evidence

dolmen a cromlech, a monument of rough stones **dolmenic**

donkey's years a very long time

donnybrook an inordinately wild brawl; a contentious dispute; a chaotic scene [from a suburb of Dublin, the former site of an unruly annual fair]

dorsaloquium a place or time in which many are talking behind people's backs **doughty** valiant

Dr. Strangelove someone who is irresponsible and rash with dangerous weapons, esp. nuclear bombs [from the 1964 British-American black comedy film Dr. Strangelove]

drachenfutter gift offered as appeasement to a wife or girlfriend upset at her mate [from German (dragon fodder)]

draconic suggestive of a dragon; Draconian

Dracula sneeze covering one's mouth with the crook of the elbow when sneezing

dragoman an interpreter or guide; a term in general use in the Levant

dragonnade a rapid and devastating military incursion or persecution

dragoon to compel submission by violent measures; to harass; to persecute; to abandon to the rage of soldiers

dreadnought the biggest or most puissant of its kind

dripstone stalactite or stalagmite; in architecture, a protective molding over a door or window that forces rain to drip away from the structure **droke** steep-sided valley

dromic or **dromical** pertaining to a footrace course or dromos, an ancient Greek racecourse and footrace

dromomania an irrational impulse to purposelessly travel or wander

droogish relating to the nature or attitudes of a member of a street gang

dryasdust a very dry, dull, or pedantic speaker or writer [from Jonas Dryasdust, a fictitious person to whom Sir Walter Scott dedicated some novels]

drygulch to murder or attack, esp. in ambush; to suddenly betray   **dubiety** doubtfulness; uncertainty; doubt

dubiosity the state of being doubtful; a doubtful statement or thing

duende (doo-EN-day) an imp; an evil or mischievous spirit; charm; charisma; the ability to attract through personal charm   **dulcifluous** flowing sweetly

dulcify to sweeten; to calm

dulciloquy a soft or sweet manner of speaking

dulcinea a mistress or girlfriend   **dulcorate** to sweeten, to make less acrimonious   **dulcoration**

duumvirate any of several branches of the executive in ancient Rome controlled by two people; a group of two officials; a union or coalition of two people

ebberman a person who tries to catch fish under bridges

ecdemic originating from outside its usual area; of foreign origin; [opposite of endemic]

echolalia neurotic, involuntary echoing of another's speech; the normal imitations of vocal sounds by a child

echopraxia involuntary imitation of another person's actions

éclat brilliant success or conspicuous achievement; notable acclamation

eclogue a pastoral poem, esp. in which shepherds are introduced conversing with each other

edaphic relating to, or determined by, soil conditions, esp. as it relates to biological forms

effleurage form of massage employing hands in smooth strokes of the skin

effluvium (pl. **effluvia**) a gaseous or vaporous emission, esp. a foul-smelling one; the act of flowing out; discharge of liquid, outlet, efflux

efflux or **effluxion** the process of flowing out; effluence;

emanation   **effulge** to shine forth; to beam

eftsoons soon afterward; in a short time

egesta excrement or waste ejected from an organism

eidetic of or pertaining to a vivid memory or mental image of perfect clarity, as though actually visible; or to one that experiences such memories

eidolon an image or representation; a form; a phantom; an apparition

eidos the unique expression of the intellect of a culture or group

eigengrau the dark gray color a human eye sees in complete darkness – due to signals from the optic nerves

einkanter a large or small rock polished by windblown sand

ejecta material which has been ejected, esp. from a volcano

eldren or **eldern** old

elevenses a midmorning snack break after breakfast but before lunch

elflock hair matted, or twisted into a knot, as if by elves

elucubrate or **lucubrate** to study or write diligently by night

elysian of or relating to Elysium; blissful

Elysium or **Elysian Fields** in Greek mythology, home of the blessed after death; paradise

emarcid in botany, wilted or limp

embacle a grouping of broken river ice

emblaze or **imblaze** kindle; set ablaze; adorn with glittering embellishments; to cause to glitter or shine; to etch or display in a bright, fiery way; to blazon or emblazon

embonpoint plumpness; "Beyond embonpoint, he'd achieved a perfect conflation twixt arse & torso"

embosk to hide something or someone with foliage or its like

embracive disposed to embrace; fond of caressing

embrangle to confuse; to entangle; to make complicated

embrocation the act of moistening and rubbing a part of the body with lotion, oil, etc.; the liquid or lotion so applied

embuggerance any hazard or obstacle, whether natural or artificial, that impedes or complicates a proposed course of action [Brit. military slang]

emmew to mew; to confine, esp. in a coop or cage

emmolient soothing

empanoply to protect with a full suit of armor

empathogen or **entactogen** a class of psychoactive drugs that produce distinctive emotional and social effects similar to those of MDMA (ecstasy)

empery wide dominion; empire; sovereignty

empressement effusive politeness or friendliness

emprise an enterprise; endeavor; adventure; "In brave pursuit of chivalrous emprise" – Spenser; the qualities which prompt one to undertake difficult and dangerous exploits; "I love thy courage yet and bold emprise; but here thy sword can do thee little stead" – Milton

empurple to tinge or dye a purple color; to discolor with purple

empyreal formed of pure fire or light; pertaining to the highest & purest region of heaven; "Go, soar with Plato to the empyreal sphere" – Pope; pure; vital; celestial; elevated

empyrean the highest region of Heaven; the home of God; paradise; the sky

emunction the act of clearing out or cleaning bodily passages, esp. blowing one's nose

encincture to surround; a girdle or cincture

enfant terrible someone with shockingly bad or unconventional behavior

enfilade a firing in the direction of the length of a trench, or a line of parapet or troops, etc.; a raking fire

engirdle surround   **engram** the supposed physical change in neural tissue caused by a memory

enhalo to surround something with a halo; to encircle; to make a saint of

enharmonic equivalency when a note, interval or key signature is equivalent to another note, interval, or key signature but is "spelled", or named differently

enmesh or **immesh** to net; to entangle; to entrap

ennead the number nine or any group of nine

ennoble to make noble; to elevate in degree, qualities, or excellence; to dignify **enow** enough

ensanguine to stain or cover with blood; to make bloody, or of a blood-red color   **ensepulcher** to entomb

ensky to exalt; to immortalize; to place in heaven or the sky

ensorcell or **ensorcel** to bewitch or enchant someone

ensoul to imbue or endow (a body) with a soul; to place or cherish in the soul

entelechy the complete realization and final form of a potential concept or function; the conditions under which a potential thing becomes actualized

entheate divinely inspired

entheogen a psychoactive substance used to induce a mystical or spiritual experience

entheomania neurotic belief that one is divinely inspired; overly passionate belief in religion

entomb to deposit in a tomb, as a dead body; to bury; to Inter; to inhume

entryism tactic by which an organization encourages members to join another organization and attempt to lure recruits or take over entirely; tactic of joining a group in order to change its policies from within

enubilate to clear from mist, clouds or obscurity

enwomb to impregnate; to bury or hide

enzone to engirdle or encircle

eoan relating to the dawn; eastern

eolation in geology, the effects wind has on various landforms   **eosophobia** fear of dawn

ephebe a young man, esp. an 18-20 year old in ancient Greece undergoing military training; a young suitor

ephemeromorph forms of life that are lower than animal or vegetable

ephemeron (pl. **ephemera**) something that is short-lived or transitory

epichorial in or of a rural area or the countryside

epichoric of or pertaining to a specific location; local

epigone a follower or disciple; any inferior imitator, esp. of a well known artist; a descendent less talented than his ancestors   **epimyth** the moral of a story

epiphenomenon a secondary state, process or activity that results from another; an additional symptom developing during the course of an illness, but not necessarily connected to it [from Greek epi- (upon, after, over) + phainomenon (that which appears)]

epithalamion a poem or song in celebration of a wedding

epithymetic of or pertaining to desire or appetite

epuration purification

equilibrist one who balances himself in unnatural positions; a balancer; a tightrope walker

equipollent having equal power or force; equivalent; in logic, having equivalent significance

ere before; sooner than   **erelong** before long; soon

eremic of or inhabiting deserts   **erewhile** some time ago

erg a large desert region of shifting sands and little or no vegetation, esp. in the Sahara; the unit of work or energy in the centimeter-gram-second system [Greek ergon (work), ultimately from Indo-European root werg (to do)]

ergasiophobia an aversion to work or a fear of being able to work properly, esp. by a surgeon

ergophobia irrational fear of working

eristic of something or someone provoking strife, controversy or discord; one who is disputatious, esp. if disputatious while using subtle and specious reasoning

erotogenic causing sexual excitation

erstwhile at one time; heretofore; formerly

erubescent becoming reddish; blushing

erumpent breaking or bursting out; bursting through a covering

esbat a gathering of witches for pleasure, to celebrate a full moon, or to discuss witch business

escadrille a small squadron, esp. of airplanes; a unit of (usually) ten or more aircraft in WWI France

escamotage conjuring; sleight of hand

eschaton literally, last thing; in theology, the end of the world

esclavage a heavy necklace of chains, beads, or jewels

esemplastic unifying; shaping separate things into one thing

esoteric intended for the specially initiated

espalier a railing or trellis upon which fruit trees or shrubs are trained, as upon a wall; a tree or row of trees so trained (espaliered as a southern meadow's edge)

esper a person or being possessing paranormal abilities or advanced mental capabilities   **esperance** hope

espial the act of espying; notice; discovery; a spy

esprit d'escalier the feeling one gets when one thinks of the things one should have said too late, after exiting a conversation; afterwit; such a remark itself

essorant in heraldry, a bird standing, with wings spread, as if about to take flight; soaring

estrapade the rearing, plunging and kicking actions of a horse trying to dislodge its rider

estrum or **estrus** or **oestrus** the periodic biological occurrence of sexual receptivity in most female mammals   **etheromania** an addiction to ether

ethos the character or fundamental values of a person, culture, or movement

eumoiriety happiness due to being innocent, good and pure **eumoirous**

eunoia literally, beautiful thinking; a state of normal mental health

euphony a pleasing or sweet sound, esp. of spoken words euphonious

euphoriant a drug which produces feelings of euphoria

euphorigenic of or pertaining to causing euphoria

euripus a much agitated strait; a narrow tract of water where the current flows strong

eustress literally, good stress; positive response to healthy levels of stress

evagation the act of wandering; excursion; a roving or rambling; digression

evanish to vanish; to disappear; to escape from sight or perception; "Or like the rainbow's lovely form, / Evanishing amid the storm" – Burns

evulsion the act of plucking or forcing an extraction

exanimate devoid of animation; spiritless; disheartened; to kill; to dishearten; to discourage

excantation disenchantment by a countercharm; using enchantment to counteract an incantation

exclaustration the return to the secular world of a monk, nun, or other religious devotee after being released from their religious vows

excreta human bodily waste excreted from the body

excursive rambling; wandering; deviating; as an excursive fancy or imagination

exedra in architecture, a semicircular recess, with stone benches; a curved bench with a high back

exigent requiring immediate aid or action; pressing; critical; demanding; exacting

exosculate to kiss; esp. to kiss repeatedly, fondly, or fervently

expiscate to fish out; to find out by skill or laborious investigation; to search out   **explaterate** to talk nonstop

exsanguine lacking blood; having lost much blood; appearing to lack blood **exsanguinate**

exsibilation the disapproving hisses of an audience

exsufflicate empty, frivolous

exurb a residential region lying beyond the suburbs of a city, esp. one with rich residents

exurbia collective term for exurb

eyeservice service or work performed only while the employer is watching

fabulist one who invents or writes fables; a liar

fain well-pleased; glad; apt; wont; fond; inclined; with joy, gladly; to be delighted

faineant (fay-nay-ah(n)) doing nothing; disinclined to work or exertion; an idler; a sluggard

fairy ring a circle of mushrooms imagined to have been made by fairies

falling rhythm rhythmic pattern where the stress falls on the first syllable of each foot

famulus (pl. **famuli**) a private secretary; a personal assistant to a scholar or magician

fanion in armies, a small flag carried with the baggage

fantast one whose manners or ideas are fantastic, impractical; visionary or dreamy **fantasticate** to make fantastic

fantastico a very strange or bizarre person

farblondjet lost; confused [Yiddish (completely lost)]

farctate the state of having overeaten

farouche sullen and shy; recalcitrant; unpolished; fiercely wild

farrago a confused mixture, esp. a mess of premises that seem logical but are not **farraginous**

fastness a fortress or castle; a remote and secret locale

fata morgana a mirage caused by temperature inversion where distant objects are distorted, esp. such a mirage in the strait between Italy and Sicily

fatidic of or related to prophecy; prophetic

fatidical having power to foretell future events; prophetic; fatiloquent; as, the fatidical oak

faveolate honeycomb; having cavities or cells, somewhat resembling those of a honeycomb; alveolate

favonian pertaining to the west wind; soft; mild; gentle [Latin favonius (the west wind)] **febricity** feverishness

feckless spiritless; weak; worthless; helpless; ineffectual

feculent abounding with dirt or excrementitious matter; muddy; covered with filth; containing or akin to feces; foul

fedayeen Arab guerrilla warriors who are willing to martyr themselves

felicific calculus an algorithm formulated by utilitarian philosopher Jeremy Bentham for calculating the amount of pleasure a specific action is likely to cause by balancing the probable pleasures and pains that it would produce

felicitous characterized by felicity; happy; prosperous; delightful; skilful; successful; appropriate

fells rocky or barren hills; moors; downs; wild fields

felsenmeer an area covered with angular boulders broken up by the freeze and thaw cycle – occurring in mountainous arctic regions on slopes less than 25 degrees [German (sea of rock)]

felucca a small, swift-sailing vessel, propelled by oars and lateen sails [Mediterranean]

feme sole any single woman, either divorced, widowed, or never married

femtosecond one quadrillionth part of a second (one-thousandth of a picosecond)

fenestral pertaining to a window or to windows

fenestrated having windows

feracious fruitful; producing abundantly; fecund

fernbrake a patch of ferns

ferity wildness; savageness; fierceness

fey magical or fairy-like; strange or otherworldly; fated; doomed; on the verge of sudden or violent death; clairvoyance or clairaudience; overrefined, precious; quaint, cute

fibril strand; a small fiber; a very slender thread; a fibrilla

fictile pliable; molded, or capable of being molded, into form by art, as clay for pottery

fictive fictitious; imaginary; feigned; counterfeit "the fount of fictive tears" – Tennyson

fifth column a clandestine group of persons inside the battle lines of a territory engaged in a conflict, who secretly sympathize with the enemy, and who engage in espionage or sabotage

filipendulous suspended by a single thread

firedrake a fire-breathing dragon; a furnace worker; a meteor

firefanged burnt

fissilingual having a forked or cleft tongue

fissiparous reproducing by spontaneous fission; tending to break into smaller pieces

fjeld high plateau in Scandinavia

flacon a small bottle, often used for keeping perfume

flagellum (pl. **flagella**) a young, flexible shoot of a plant, esp. the long trailing branch of a vine; a long, whip-like cilium; a whip **flagellate** to whip; to scourge; to flog

flammeous pertaining to, consisting of, or resembling, flame

flammiferous producing flame

flammule a little flame, esp. one associated with Chinese and Japanese gods and other sacred beings

flaneur an aimless idler; a loafer; a soulful urban wanderer; one who strolls to savor the city

flatus a breath; a puff of wind; gas generated in the stomach or other bodily cavity; flatulence

flaughter to flutter or flicker; to frighten; a fluttering movement **flavescent** yellowish or turning yellow

fledge to furnish with feathers necessary for flight; to care for a bird until able of fly; to fit with feathers, esp. as an arrow

fledgling a young bird with just developed flight feathers; an immature, naïve or inexperienced person

fleshment the excitement one feels in a successful beginning

fleer to deride; to mock; to jeer; to make faces in contempt

flense to strip the blubber or the skin from a whale, seal, etc.

fleshling a person devoted to fleshly things

fleshspades fingernails **fleuron** a flower-shaped ornament

flexion a bend; a fold; the act of bending

flexuose or **flexuous** having windings and turnings; undulating; wavering; flickering

flexure a curve, turn, or fold; the act of bending or flexing

flibbertigibbet an offbeat, skittish person, esp. such a young woman; a flighty person; someone regarded as silly, irresponsible, or scatterbrained, esp. someone who gossips

flinders splinters or fragments

flinty like flint; very hard, not impressible; as a flinty heart; cruel; unmerciful; inexorable

flittermouse or **fluttermouse** a bat; flindermouse

flivver an automobile, esp. one which is old and inexpensive

floccipend to consider worthless [Latin floccus (tuft of wool) + pendere (to weigh or consider)]

flocculent woolly   **florescence** a bursting into flower; a blossoming

floricomous having the head adorned with flowers

floriferous producing flowers

foudroyant dazzling; having an awesome and overwhelming effect, esp. suddenly

flounce to spring, turn, or twist with sudden effort or violence; to struggle, as a horse in mire; to flounder; a narrow piece of cloth sewed to a petticoat, frock or gown

fluctisonant having the sound of rolling waves

fluminous pertaining to rivers; abounding in streams

flummery a light kind of food, formerly made of flour or meal; something insipid, or not worth having; empty compliment; trash; nonsense

flummox to exasperate; to confuse; to fluster; to flabbergast

flyleaf a blank or specially printed page at the front or back of a book

fogbow faint rainbow-like arc of light sometimes seen in fog opposite the sun; sundog

foehn a warm dry wind blowing down the side of a mountain in northern and central Europe

foetor or **fetor** a very bad odor

folderol or **falderal** nonsense; foolish talk

Folketing parliament of Denmark

foo reality substitute   **foothot** hastily; immediately; instantly

footling inept; trivial

foozle to bungle   **forbearance** the exercise of patience; long suffering; tolerance

force majeure an overwhelming force; an unavoidable circumstance, esp. one that prevents someone from fulfilling a legal obligation

forcemeat meat, fish or poultry chopped fine and highly seasoned

foregleam an antecedent or premonitory gleam; a dawning light

forenoon the early part of the day, from morning to noon

foretoken to presignify; to presage; to prognosticate; a warning

forfex a pair of scissors **forjeskit** weary and jaded

formicary an ant colony or hill **formic** relating to ants

formicate to swarm like ants

forswink to exhaust by labor; overwork

forwhy because; wherefore

fossa a long, narrow, shallow depression on a planet, moon or other extraterrestrial body

foulard a thin, washable material of silk, or silk and cotton

fourth estate the press, collectively

foxfire bioluminescence from a fungus that grows on decaying wood

frabjous fabulous, joyous, great, wonderful [from Lewis Carroll's poem Jabberwocky]

frankalmoigne a tenure by which a religious corporation holds lands given to them and their successors in perpetuity **frass** insect excrement

freebooter one who plunders or pillages without the authority of national warfare; a member of a predatory band; a pillager; a buccaneer; a sea robber; a pirate

freemartin sterile female calf, born with a bull twin; lesbian; hermaphrodite

fremescence the sound of a crowd of people trending toward displeasure

fremitus a noticeable vibration, esp. as felt on the chest when one speaks or coughs

frescade a cool walk, esp. with attendant breeze; a shady place good for relaxing

frigiferous bearing or bringing cold

frigorific causing to cool or chill; freezing

frisson a sudden surge of excitement; a shiver [old French fricon (a trembling)]

fritinancy the chirping or croaking of insects

frore frozen; very cold

frostwork any naturally occurring intricate pattern of ice crystals

frottage the practice of two consenting humans rubbing body parts together to obtain sexual gratification, both parties usually being clothed

frotteur someone who participates in frottage

frowzy or **frowsty** having a dingy, neglected, and scruffy appearance; having a musty odor

fug heavy, musty, and unpleasant air, esp. in a poorly-ventilated space **fuggy**

fugacious flying; fleeing away; lasting but a short time; volatile; evanescent; in botany, withering or falling off early

fugleman one who leads a group, company, or party, esp. in military exercises [German]

fulgid shining; glittering; dazzling

fulgor splendor; dazzling brightness

fulgural of, like or pertaining to lightning

fulgurous or **fulgurant** resembling lightning; full of lightning

fuliginous sooty; dusky

fulmar polar seabird   **fulmen** lightning

fulminant exploding or detonating; suddenly severe or intense

fulmineous of or pertaining to thunder

fulminate to explode; to speak or write in anger

fulsome tactless; overzealous; excessively flattering as to be insincere; abundant; copious; fully developed, mature

fulvous tawny; reddish-brown

fumifugist one who, or that which, drives away smoke or fumes

fumulus a very thin cloud resembling a veil, esp. one formed of water droplets from the plume of a cooling tower, etc.

fundus the bottom or the depths of something; in anatomy, the base of any hollow organ

funebral or **funebrial** pertaining to funerals; funereal

furibund raging; furious; choleric

fusillade a simultaneous discharge of firearms

fustian a coarse twilled cotton fabric; an inflated style of writing; bombast   **futhark** the Germanic runic alphabet

futilitarian having the opinion that all human activity is futile

futurition the state of being to come or exist hereafter; futurity

gabble to talk fast, or without meaning; to prate; to jabber; to utter inarticulate sounds with rapidity

gadzookery the heavy use of archaic speech, esp. in historical novels

galligaskins leggings or loose trousers

gallinipper large mosquito

gambrinous having a belly full of beer

gamely in a plucky manner; spiritedly

gammerstang a tall and awkward human, esp. a female

gangrel wanderer; vagrant; vagabond; a tall awkward man

garboil tumult; disturbance; disorder; uproar

gardyloo! an old warning cry when throwing water, slops, etc., from windows in Edinburgh

gargalesthesia the sensation commonly associated with tickling

garrison finish the end of a contest in which the winner comes from behind at the last second [named after an American horse race jockey]

garth a grassy yard; a garden; a clearing

gasconade a boast or boasting; a vaunt; a bravado

gatefold an oversized page folded into a book or magazine; a foldout

gaucherie an awkward or socially unacceptable action or remark; clumsiness; boorishness **gaucheries**

gault heavy clay   **gawp** to stare stupidly or rudely; gawk

gazump to swindle or extort

gegenschein a faint brightening visible in the night sky's antisolar point (area furthest from the sun) caused by sunlight backscattered by interplanetary dust; counterglow

[German, countershine]

geist ghost; spirit (as of an age, a group, etc); trait of being intelligent or motivated

gelasin dimple on the cheek that usually appears when someone smiles

gelastic pertaining to laughter; causing laughter

gelogenic causing laughter

geloscopy divination by means of laughter

gemel coupled; paired or occurring in pairs

gemelliparous producing, or having given birth to, twins

gement groaning in sorrow

gemma a leaf bud, as distinguished from a flower bud; bud from which a new plant could grow

gemutlich having an atmosphere of amiability; friendly and pleasant

generative procreative; having the power of generating, originating, or producing

genetrix mother; a female ancestor or progenitor

genophobia fear of having sex

georama a hollow globe of the Earth designed to be viewed from within

georgic relating to agriculture or rural affairs; a poem relating to same; rural; "Long he bathed in the georgic mansuetude of that alpestrine aestivation..."

geoselenic pertaining to the Earth and the Moon

gestalt (pl. **gestalten**) shape; form; a collection of real or symbolic entities that creates a unified concept or pattern which is greater than the sum of its parts

ghat a mountain range or pass; a path or stairway leading to a river or ford [India]

ghostshipping gliding through or completely ignoring one's responsibilities in a job, relationship, etc.

gibber to speak rapidly and inarticulately; to prattle; a boulder

gibbosity state of being convex or protuberant

gibbous convex; protuberant; the moon is gibbous between half and full phase

gigantomachy in Greek mythology, the symbolic struggle between the Olympian gods (the cosmic order) and the Giants (the nether forces of Chaos)

glabella the space between the eyebrows on a human [Latin glabellus (bald, hairless)] **glabrous** smooth

glacis a gentle slope, or a smooth, gently sloping bank

gladsome pleased; joyful; cheerful; causing joy or pleasure

glair any viscous or slimy substance, esp. egg white used for industrial purposes **glaireous**

Glasgow kiss a headbutt **glebous** turfy; cloddy; earthy

gleed a live or glowing coal **glim** a light; a glimpse; to shine

glisk a glimpse; a gleam of light [Scottish]

glister glittering or sparkling **glistering**

glitterati the beautiful people; the rich & famous; highly fashionable people prominent in the public eye

gloriole halo

glossa the tongue, esp. the tongue of an insect

gloze to flatter; to fawn; to talk smoothly; to palliate

glozing flattering; wheedling; specious representation

gnar to snarl; to growl

gnomic of, or relating to, gnomes; uttering or containing maxims; aphoristic

gnosis the deeper wisdom; knowledge of spiritual truth, such as claimed by the Gnostics, attainable by faith or insight

goatish lustful; resembling a goat in any quality; of a rank smell; foolish

gobbet a lump or chunk, esp. of raw meat; an extract of text or image, esp. a quotation, provided as context for analysis, translation or discussion in an examination

gobemouche naive person; one who keeps his mouth open; a boor; a silly and credulous person [literally, a fly swallower]

godwottery affectedly archaic or elaborate speech writing; an affected or over-elaborate style of gardening or attitude toward gardens [from the 1876 poem "My Garden" by Thomas Edward Brown, which begins: "A garden is a lovesome thing, God wot"]

goetic pertaining to black magic or necromancy

Golden Horde Mongol invaders of eastern Europe in the 13th century

golden mean the way of wisdom and safety between extremes; sufficiency without excess; moderation

golgotha hill near Jerusalem where Jesus was crucified; a place of burial, suffering, or sacrifice

goliard a 12th and 13th century wandering student, whose convivial lifestyle included minstrelsy

goluptious splendid, delightful, magnificent

gonfalon a banner or standard of the middle ages

gongoozler a person who enjoys watching activity on the canals in the United Kingdom, or who simply has an interest in canals and the canal life; an idle spectator of any event

gonkulator a piece of equipment that in reality serves no useful purpose; also can be used in place of an actual technical term for any particularly loathed mechanical device or computer hardware

goobermensch someone who thinks he is, but very much isn't, an ubermensch

gorbellied fat; corpulent; possessing a protruding belly

gorcock the moor cock, or red grouse
"Above the daedal wood, thick with gorcock and brocket..."

gorget a piece of armor defending the throat; an ornament for the neck; a necklace

gorgon an intimidating, ugly, or disgusting woman; anything hideous or horrid

gorgonize to have the effect of a Gorgon upon; to turn to stone; to petrify; to paralyze [after Gorgon, any of the three monstrous sisters Stheno, Euryale, and Medusa in Greek mythology who could turn to stone anyone who looked into their eyes]

gork a vegetable, as in a severely mentally or physically handicapped person [perhaps from the slang term gorked (anesthetized)]; a patient with an undiagnosed ailment [short for "God only really knows"]

gormandism gluttony

gormless dull or stupid; lacking intelligence or discernment; inexperienced; very naive

gossamer a fine, filmy substance like cobwebs floating in the air in calm weather; any very thin gauze-like fabric; anything light, thin, airy, or unsubstantial

götterdämmerung in Germanic mythology, the destruction of the gods in a final battle with evil forces; any cataclysmic downfall, esp. of a regime or an institution [German Götterdämmerung (twilight of the gods)]

gowpen a bowl made of two hands cupped together

goyim plural for gentile [Yiddish]

grabble to grope; to feel or search with the hands

graben in geology, an elongated section of the Earth's crust that has moved lower relative to the surrounding blocks by tectonic processes; a rift valley   **gracile** slender

gramarye necromancy, magic; occult learning

granitic like granite in composition, color, etc.; consisting of granite; completely unyielding

grappa an Italian, grape-based brandy

graustark an imaginary place of idealized adventure and romance; a piece of writing that includes similar idealized, romantic elements [from the imaginary country said to be in Eastern Europe in the novel Graustark]   **graustarkian**

gravamen in law, the foundation or essence of a complaint

gravid being with child; heavy with young; pregnant; fruitful; as, a gravid uterus

gravida a pregnant woman [referred to as gravida one during first pregnancy, gravida two during the second, etc.]

greenth greenness; verdure

greenware pottery that has been shaped, but not yet fired

gregal pertaining to, or like, a flock   **gregatim** in flocks

gremial of or pertaining to the lap or bosom; intimate

gridelin gray-violet color

griffin fanciful beast with an eagle's head and wings and a lion's body

griffonage bad handwriting, esp. when illegible; cacography

grimalkin an old cat, esp. a she-cat

grimthorpe to remodel a building poorly, ignoring its character and/or history

grinagog a person who is always grinning

grisaille in fine arts, a decorative painting in gray monochrome   **grith** peace; security; agreement

groak to look at longingly, esp. at someone eating while hoping for an offering

groggery a shop or room where strong liquors are sold and drunk; a dramshop

grok to have a complete intuitive understanding of something [from the Martian language in Robert Heinlein's Stranger in a Strange Land where the word is described as coming from the word for "to drink" and, figuratively, "to drink in all available aspects of reality"]

growler a small, mostly submerged, iceberg

growlery a place of solitary retreat for periods of ill humor

grufted dirty; befouled

grume a thick, viscid fluid; a clot, as of blood

gruntling a young pig   **gundygut** a glutton

gunkhole small cove with suitable anchorage for small boats

gurge a whirlpool; to engulf

gutterblood a person of inferior breeding; one of the common rabble

guttersnipe a species of bird; someone who collects useful garbage from gutters; a dirty child dressed in rags

gynotikolobomassophilia the desire to nibble on a woman's earlobes

gyromancy divination where someone walks on a circle of letters until so dizzy they fall

gyrovague a wondering monk with no home monastery [Late Latin gyrovagus gyro- (circle) + vagus (wandering)]

gyrus a convoluted ridge between grooves; a convolution;

as, the gyri of the brain   **gyve** shackle, esp. for legs

haboob a violent sandstorm or dust storm, esp. in North Africa or Arabia

habromania psychosis featuring delightful and blithe delusions; the euphoria of an ill mind

haecceity a term to express individuality or singleness [Latin – literally, this-ness]

haemal pertaining to the blood or blood vessels

haematic or **hematic** of, pertaining to, affecting or containing blood; blood-colored

hagridden ridden by a witch; tormented by nightmares or unreasonable dreads

haimish or **heimish** home-like, friendly, folksy [Yiddish heymish]

hakenkreuz swastika; literally "hooked cross"

halcyon pertaining to or resembling the halcyon, a bird of myth said to nest on the sea and calm the weather during the winter solstice; calm; quiet; peaceful   **halcyonian**

halidom holiness; sanctity; sacred oath; sacred things; sanctuary

halitus the breath; exhaled breath   **hallux** big toe

hamada or **hammada** a type of desert landscape with a stony or rocky surface and little or no sand

hamadryad in Greek & Roman mythology, a wood nymph whose life ended when the particular tree she inhabited, usually an oak, died

hamartia the protagonist's tragic flaw in a literary tragedy

hamate hooked; hamous   **hame** harness collar for a draught horse (or a human slave)

hapaxanthous a plant that flowers only once, then dies

haptic relating to, or based on the sense of touch; tactile [Greek haptesthai (to touch)]

hariolate to prophesy; to foretell

harmattan a dry, hot wind, prevailing on the Atlantic coast of Africa, blowing from the interior or Sahara [Arabic haram (forbidden thing)]

harmonic progression or **harmonic sequence** in mathematics, the reciprocals of an arithmetic progression

harpagon grappling hook **harridan** old, scolding woman

haruspex priest in ancient Rome who inspected animals' entrails as a form of divination

hawkshaw detective **haycock** hay heaped in a conical pile

heartsome cheerful; lively; merry

hebetic of or related to youth or to puberty

hebetude dullness, stupidity

hecatomb any great sacrifice; a great number of people, animals or things, esp. as sacrificed or destroyed; a large amount **hedonics** the ethical study of pleasure

hedonometer or **hedonimeter** a device used to measure happiness or pleasure

heimganger a person who stays at home

heliophilous fond or attracted to sunlight

heliosis sunstroke; scorching of plants by the sun; exposure to the sun

heliotrope heliotrope purple; a grayish purple color

helliferocious extremely ferocious

helve handle of an ax, or ax-like tool

hemal or **hemic** relating to blood

hematic relating to or containing blood

hemicycle a half circle or semicircle; a semicircular place, such as an arena, room, etc.

hemidemisemiquaver in music, a 1/64 note

hemipygic possessing one, rather than two, buttocks (or, figuratively, half-arsed) **henotic** harmonizing; irenic

heptamerous consisting of seven parts; having the parts in sets of sevens **hermetic** of or pertaining to alchemy

heroic couplet two rhyming lines of verse, each with five feet of two syllables with the stress on the second syllable (iambic pentameter)

Hesperus Venus, when she is the evening star

hesperian western; occidental

hesternal pertaining to yesterday [Latin hesternus]

hetaeric like a particularly refined ancient Greek courtesan

heteroclite abnormal, anomalous

heuristic serving to discover or find out

hibernaculum winter home or retreat

hibernacle that which serves for protection or shelter in winter; winter quarters for human, animal, or plant

hibernicism an Irish idiom, mode of speech, or custom

hidrosis excretion of sweat; perspiration, esp. when excessive [Greek hidros (sweat)]   **hidrotic** exuding sweat; sudorific

hie to hasten; to go in haste

hiemal or **hibernal** belonging or relating to winter; wintry

hierophant the presiding priest who initiated candidates in the Eleusinian mysteries; one who teaches the mysteries and duties of religion

hierophobia a fear of sacred things or people

highbinder a corrupt politician; a swindler

Himalayan resembling the Himalayas; very large

hindermate a friend or companion who is a somehow a hindrance

hippic of, like, relating or belonging to horses or horse racing

hippopotomonstrosesquipedalian pertaining to a truly, very, very long word or words

hircosity condition of being like a goat; lewdness

hirple to walk haltingly or lamely

hispid covered with strong hairs, bristles or minute spines

hist a word commanding silence; equivalent to hush, be silent [interjection]

hitherside the nearer side; this side of someone or something

hodiernal of this day; belonging to the present day

holobenthic of animals, completing the entire life cycle in the deep ocean

holocryptic incapable of being deciphered

holt a piece of woodland, esp. a woody hill

homocentric having the same center or focal point; focused on humans; having a homosexual bias or basis

horrescent showing horror; shuddering

horripilate having one's hair stand on end; experiencing goose bumps or piloerection

horripilation fear or cold causing the erection of the hair of the head or body of many mammals

horrisonant or **horrisonous** sounding dreadfully; uttering a terrible sound

hortative or **hortatory** encouraging; giving exhortation; advisory; exhortative

hortulan of, like, relating to, or belonging to a garden

hotspur a violent, passionate, or rash man; violent; impetuous

houri in Islam, a nymph in the form of a beautiful virgin supposed to dwell in Paradise for the enjoyment of the faithful; any voluptuous, beautiful woman [from Persian]

hoyden or **hoiden** tomboy; a saucy, boisterous or high-spirited girl

hwyl emotional intensity stirring motivation and energy, esp. toward poetry, song or eloquence [Welsh]

hyaline a poetic term for the sea or the atmosphere; glassy; resembling glass; consisting of glass; transparent, like crystal **hyalescent** becoming hyaline

hyetal rainy; of or pertaining to rain; descriptive of the distribution of rain, or of rainy regions

hyle the first matter of the cosmos, from which the four elements arose, according to the doctrines of Empedocles and Aristotle; generic term for matter in early philosophy

hylephobia fear of materialism

hylopathism the doctrine that matter is sentient

hylophobia fear of forests

hymeneal of or pertaining to marriage or a wedding; a hymn or poem in honor of a wedding **hypactic** purgative

hypaethral open-air, outdoor, exposed to the sky

hyperborean northern; belonging to, or inhabiting, a region in very far north; very cold

hyperhedonia feeling great pleasure from something common or mundane

hypertrophication making a trophy of something in an

extreme or neurotic manner

hypnogenesis the process of inducing sleep or a hypnotic state **hypnogenic**

hypnogogic or **hypnagogic** of or relating to the state of consciousness just before sleep; sleep-inducing; applied to the illusions of one who is half asleep

hypnopompic referring to the state of consciousness before becoming completely awake [Greek hypnos (sleep) + pompe (sending away)]

hypogeal existing or growing underground

hypogeum an underground room or cavern

hypomania a mild form of mania, esp. the phase of several mood disorders characterized by euphoria or hyperactivity

hypostatize to make into, or regarded as, a separate and distinct substance; to construct a contextually subjective and complex abstraction, idea, or concept into a universal object without regard to nuance or change in character

ianthine violet-colored

icarian soaring too high for safety; adventurous in flight; relating to any overly ambitious venture that ends in utter failure [after Icarus in Greek mythology who plunged to his death after flying so high the sun melted the wax in his hand-crafted wings]

iceblink a bright appearance or yellowish glare above an ice field; a coastal ice face

ichor in mythology, an ethereal fluid flowing through the veins of the gods in place of blood

ichthyic fish-like; pertaining to fish

ideogram an original, pictorial element of writing; a symbol that represents no sound, but only an idea; a symbol used for convenience or abbreviation

ideopraxist one who is impelled to action by an idea, or who works to bring an idea to fruition

idioglossia a unique language, such as developed between children, esp. twins

idiomorphic or **idiomorphous** having a unique form

ignescent emitting sparks of fire when struck with steel; having a volatile mood **ignify** to form into fire

ignis fatuus a phosphorescent light that appears, in the night, over marshy ground, supposed to be caused by the decomposition of animal or vegetable substances – also called friar's lantern or will-o'-the-wisp; a misleading influence; a decoy

ignipotent presiding or having power over fire; fiery

ignivomous vomiting fire, as an ignivomous volcano

illapse a gliding in; an immission or entrance of one thing into another; a sudden descent or attack

illaqueate to ensnare, entrap, entangle, or otherwise catch

illation the act or process of inferring from premises or reasons; perception of the connection between ideas; that which is inferred; inference; deduction; conclusion

illative relating to, dependent on, or denoting, illation; inferential; conclusive

illeism the practice of referring to oneself in the third person

illimitable incapable of being limited or bounded; immeasurable; limitless; boundless

illiquation the melting or dissolving of one thing into another

ill-starred fated to be unfortunate; unlucky

illuminant something that illuminates; something light-giving

illuminism the belief in a special, personal enlightenment not accessible by humanity at large

illutation mud bath **imaginal** characterized by imagination; imaginative; relating to the imagination

imago idealized mental image; the final stage of an insect's metamorphoses

imbraid, embraid or **upbraid** to braid, as hair

imbricate to place overlapping one another

imbrication an overlapping of the edges, like that of tiles

imbrue to wet or moisten; to soak; to drench, esp. in blood; to stain

imbrute to degrade to the state of a brute; to make brutal; "The soul grows clotted by contagion, imbodies, and imbrutes, till she quite lose / The divine property of her first being." – Milton

immarcescible unfading; imperishable; lasting

immaterialism in philosophy, the doctrine that external bodies may be reduced to mind and ideas in a mind; any doctrine opposed to materialism or phenomenalism, esp. a system that maintains the immateriality of the soul; idealism

immiseration to make miserable, esp on a large scale; impoverishment

immix to mix; to mingle; to commingle **immixture**

immortelle dried flowers; everlasting

immure to enclose within walls, or as within walls; to shut up; to imprison; to entomb

imparadise to put in a state like paradise; to make supremely happy; to enrapture; to make somewhere into a paradise; "imparadised in one another's arms" – Paradise Lost

impavid fearless **impeccant** sinless; impeccable; faultless

impedimenta things which impede or hinder progress; encumbrances; baggage

imperium an empire; absolute power

imperseverant not persevering; fickle; thoughtless

impleach to pleach; to interweave or intertwine

implead to sue; to accuse

implex intricate; entangled; complicated; complex

implumous having no plumes or feathers

improvidence lack of foresight; a failure to provide for needs of the future **improvident**

imputrescible immune to decay **inamorato** a male lover

inamorata a woman in love; a mistress

incalescent becoming warmer, or more ardent; heating up

incantatory dealing with enchantment; magical; chanting to cast spells **incogitant** thoughtless; inconsiderate

incommode to inconvenience **incommodious**

incompossible not capable of joint existence; incompatible

incurious not curious or inquisitive; without care for or interest in; inattentive

infaust not favorable; unlucky; unpropitious; sinister

infracaninophile one who's wont to support or champion the underdog   **ingle** a fire, esp. a log fire; a fireplace

inglenook a nook or corner near an open fireplace

inglorious not glorious; not bringing honor or glory; shameful; disgraceful; ignominious; "Death is nothing, but to live defeated and inglorious is to die daily." – Napolean

inhume to bury; to inter

inkhorn a small bottle of horn formerly used for holding ink; pedantic; obscurely scholarly

inly internal; interior; secret; completely

inselberg or **monadnock** an isolated rock hill, knob, ridge, or small mountain rising abruptly from a surrounding plain [German Insel (island) + Berg (mountain)]

insouciant careless; heedless; blithely unconcerned; nonchalant; indifferent

inspissate to thicken or bring to greater consistence, as fluids by evaporation

insufflate to project breath onto or into; to blow on

insuperable incapable of being passed over; insurmountable

integument in anatomy, a covering such as skin or a membrane; the skin of seeds or shells of crustaceous animals; any covering, coating or enclosure

intempestive out of season; untimely; inopportune

interabang or **interrobang** punctuation that combines a question mark and exclamation point

interamnian situated between rivers

intercolline situated between hills, esp. applied to valleys lying between volcanic cones

interfenestration the space between two windows

intergrade to pass from one state to another in stages

interjacent lying or being between or among; intervening, as interjacent isles

interjaculate to interject or interrupt in ejaculation; to ejaculate parenthetically

interlacustrine situated between lakes

interlard to mix fat with lean; to interpose; to insert between; to mix or mingle, esp. to introduce that which is foreign or irrelevant

interlucation act of thinning a wood to let in light

interlucent shining between

intermontane between or among mountains

internecine mutually destructive

interpellate to question formally

interpunct middot; interpoint; a punctuation mark consisting of a centered dot   **interscribe** to write between

interstice a space between things closely set, or between the parts which compose a whole; a crack; a crevice; a hole; an interval

intervale a low-lying, flat piece of land, esp. straddling a river

intramundane within the material world; opposite of extramundane

intrapreneur a company employee who is encouraged to work independently, thereby increasing innovation, revitalization, and diversity

invidious enviable; likely to incur or produce ill will, or to provoke envy; injurious

invious pathless; untrodden; impassable

involute difficult to understand; complicated; intricate; rolled inward spirally

involution entanglement; intricacy; a spiraling inwards

ipso facto by the very fact itself

irenic promoting peace; conciliatory, non-confrontational; peaceful [Greek eirene (peace) from the goddess of the same name] **irenical**

iridian of or pertaining to the iris or rainbow

ironbound bound as with iron; rugged; as, an ironbound coast; rigid; unyielding

iron-hearted cruel; pitiless   **isangelous** equal to the angels

iscariot surname of the Judas that betrayed Jesus; any traitor **iscariotic**

isinglass gelatin used as a clarifying agent and adhesive; mica or similar material in thin, transparent sheets

islesman someone who lives on a solitary island, or esp. on a island within a group   **islomania** an obsession for islands

isness the quality of being; existence as something

isobront in meteorology, a line on a weather chart signifying simultaneous storm development

isochroous uniform in color; mono-colored

ivorine like ivory in texture or color; white and smooth

izles sparks or embers floating out of a chimney

izzard an old word for the letter Z

izzat public esteem; honor, pride, dignity

jabberwock a playful imitation of language; nonsense or nonsense verse; gibberish

jactancy boastfulness; vainglory; a bragging

jactation boasting; bragging

jacquerie a revolt by the peasant class

jaggery unrefined brown sugar

janiform having two faces; resembling the two-faced god, Janus

janissary member of an elite, highly loyal group of supporters

Janus-faced two-faced   **jape** to mock; to jest

jasperated mixed with jasper, as a jasperated agate

jawhole sewer entrance; a hole where sewage is tossed [Scottish]

jebel or **djebel** hill or mountain [Arabic]; "Otherways wesways like that provost scoffing bedoueen the jebel and the jpysian sea" – Finnegans Wake

jentacular pertaining to breakfast

Jericho a very distant place, as in the phrase "go to Jericho" [after Jericho, an ancient city northwest of the Dead Sea]

jimjams slang for delirium tremens; slang for pajamas; extreme nervousness; jitters

jink to make a quick, sudden, evasive turn

jiva in Hinduism, the essence of the individual soul

jnana knowledge gained through meditation; pure awareness free of conceptual thinking

jobbernowl a blockhead [French jobard (stupid, gullible)]

Jotunheim in Norse mythology, home of the giants

jovialist one who lives a jovial life; one who is convivial

jugulate to stop something using extreme measures; to cut the throat

jument a beast, esp. a beast of burden [Latin jumentum (beast of burden)]

jumentous smelling like a beast of burden, or like horse urine

Junoesque like the goddess Juno in having a stately bearing and regal beauty; statuesque

Ka in ancient Egyptian religion, an aspect of the individual, or soul, believed to live within the body and survive death

kafkaesque complex or illogical in a disorienting, surreal, or nightmarish manner [after the Czech author Franz Kafka, who depicted such worlds in his writings]

kairos a favorable time for a decision or action; an opportune moment [Greek (opportunity)]   **kakidrosis** body odor

kakistocracy government by the worst people

kalewife female greengrocer

kalology aesthetics; the study of beauty

kalon ideal perfect beauty; deeper beauty that is more than superficial

kalopsia the delusion that things are more beautiful than they really are

kalyptra in ancient Greece, a thin veil commonly worn by women over their hair

kame a short, steep ridge of glacially deposited sand and gravel [Scottish]

karuna universal, loving compassion [Sanskrit karuna (compassion)]

katabasis a downward journey; a journey to the underworld; a military retreat   **katabatic** downward moving

katzenjammer hangover; anguish; depression; clamor; uproar

keening intense sorrowful wailing at a wake [Scottish]

kef or **kif** any drug capable of producing euphoria; a state of dreamy or euphoric drug-induced repose

keld a well or spring; a deep and calm part of a river

kelpie in Celtic mythology, a mischievous shape-shifting spirit, often in the form of a horse, believed to haunt rivers and lochs in Scotland and warn of, or sometimes assist in, drownings

kenning a far off view, esp. at sea; as far as one can see (about 20 miles at sea); wee portion

kenspeckle having so marked an appearance as to be easily recognized

kenosis Christ's voluntary divestment of his God-like form to become a man [Greek kenosis (an emptying)]

keraunoscopia divination by observing thunder

kerfuffle a commotion or tumult

kermes type of Mediterranean insect used to make red dye; bright red dye so made

khamsin a hot, perhaps sand-filled, Saharan wind (Egypt)

khor a seasonally dry watercourse in the Middle East

kindergraph a photograph of a child

kinderspiel a play or musical performed by children

kirkbuzzer a thief that robs churches

kith friends and acquaintances; kindred

klangfarbe timbre or tone color; the quality of a musical note, sound or tone that distinguishes different types of sound production

knackered quite tired

knighthead nautical, a timber used for bowsprit support

knurl a contorted knot in wood; a cross-grained protuberance; to provide with ridges to assist the grasp, as in the edge of a flat knob

kraken sea monster in Norwegian lore;
"Far far beneath in the abysmal sea,/His ancient, dreamless, uninvaded sleep/The Kraken sleepeth" – Tennyson

krans or **krantz** a cliff's overhang; a very steep rock wall surrounding a valley

krobylos in ancient Greece, a knot of hair on top or behind the head

krummholz trees in subarctic and subalpine treeline areas that are deformed by exposure to cold winds and tend to grow much nearer the ground then they otherwise would [German krumm (crooked, bent, twisted) and Holz (wood)]

Kummerspeck excess weight gained from emotional overeating [German Kummer (grief) and Speck (bacon)]

kvelling to express happiness, joy, or pride, esp. in satisfaction of one or more family members

labellum the lower petal of an orchid, often curiously shaped; "When labellum quiver, and moist lotus quake..."

lachrymal or **lacrimal** relating to tears

lacuscular of, like, relating to, or inhabiting small pools

lacustrine of or relating to lakes

lahar a volcanic mud flow [from Javanese lahar (lava)]

laic of or pertaining to a layman or the laity; a layman

lallation the incorrect pronunciation of "r" so that it sounds like an "l"; baby-talk or gibberish

lambent brushing or flickering gently over a surface; glowing or luminous but lacking heat; exhibiting lightness or brilliance of wit; clever or witty without unkindness

lambative taken by licking with the tongue, esp. a medicine so taken

lamia a female demon; a monster capable of assuming the human female form, said to devour humans or suck their blood; a vampire; a sorceress; a witch

lammergeyer long-winged vulture of Europe, Africa & India; also called bearded vulture

landloper or **landleaper** a wanderer; one who roams about the country; vagabond   **langlaufer** a cross-country skier

languor state of body or mind caused by exhaustion of strength and characterized by a languid feeling; feebleness; lassitude; laxity; listlessness; weariness **languorous**

lanneret male falcon; a male lanner, used in falconry

lanugo soft woolly hair covering the mammal fetus, shed in humans before or soon after birth; fine, soft hairs covering a leaf, an insect, etc.   **lapideous** stony

lapidescent becoming stone; substance capable of petrifying

lardaceous consisting of or resembling lard

largifical generous; ample; liberal

larruping to beat; to spank; very or excellent (slang)

laurence a shimmering above a hot surface, such as a road, from irregular refraction of light

lavaliere pendant, usually jeweled, worn around the neck

lavatic or **lavic** like or composed of lava

layette collection of things needed to meet a newborn baby's material needs

laystall an area where cattle are kept before taken to market; a place where dung is piled

lea a meadow; a grassy field [Old English leah (meadow) and ultimately from Indo-European leuk (light) – root of other words such as lunar, lunatic, light, lightning, lucid, illuminate, illustrate, translucent, lux, and lynx]

lecanoscopy a form of self-hypnosis wherein one stares into a pool, or basin of water

legerity lightness; nimbleness; agility

leggiadrous graceful; elegant; pleasing

leister a barbed spear or trident used to catch fish

leitmotif or **leitmotiv** in music, a melodic passage or phrase, esp. in Wagnerian opera, associated with a specific character, situation, or element; a dominant and recurring theme, as in a novel

lemurian like or relating to the hypothetical land, or continent, Lemuria supposedly having existed in the Indian Ocean, of which Madagascar is a remnant; lemur-like; lemurine

lenify to assuage; to soften; to mitigate; to alleviate

lenitive capable of easing pain or of soothing; that which softens or mitigates; that which tends to allay passion, excitement, or pain; a palliative

lentic in ecology, living in still waters

lepid pleasant, jocose; charming

lepidopterous in entomology, having scaly wings; relating or akin to moths or butterflies

leptodactylous having fine, slender toes or fingers

levigate to make smooth; to polish; to grind into powder

levin lightning; a flash of lightning; a thunderbolt; any bright light or flash

lexiconophilist collector of word books

lickerish eager; greedy to swallow; eager to taste or enjoy; lecherous; lusty

lickpenny a devourer or absorber of money; "Law is a lickpenny" – Sir Walter Scott

limacine of, resembling or pertaining to slugs

limax a genus of air-breathing mollusks which includes the common garden slug **limbus** in anatomy, a border

limen in psychology, a threshold, esp. the point where a psychological or physiological effect begins to occur

limerance or **limerence** the initial rush of romantic love; the state of being in love **limicolous** living in mud

limoniad or **limniad** meadow nymph **limous** muddy; slimy

lineament distinctive feature

lingula tongue-like object **lingulate** tongue-shaped

lissome easily bent; supple; lithe; thin; graceful; limber

liquate to melt **liquescent** becoming liquid

literatus a member of the literati

llano a spacious, grassy, nearly treeless plain, esp. one in Latin America **lochan** a small loch

lochetic waiting for prey to ambush, esp. said of insects

locust years a period of economic hardship [coined by Winston Churchill to refer to 1931-1935 in Britain, after "the years that the locust hath eaten" – Book of Joel]

logodaedalus a person skilled in wordcraft, or in using words

logolepsy an obsession with words

logolept a person with a mania or obsession for words; verbivore, logophile **logomancy** divination using words

logophile lover of words **logorrhea** an excessive flow of words; uncontrollable talkativeness

lollop to walk with a bounce; to loll

longanimity being calm in adversity; patience; long-suffering

longueur the most boring part of a book or story

lorica in zoology, a protective shell, such as a carapace

lorica plumata type of Roman armor; a mail shirt with small feather-like scales

lotic in ecology, of or living in actively flowing water

lotophagous lotus-eating; lazy; day-dreamy

louche (LOOSH) of dubious taste or morality; decadent; disreputable in an appealing way

lovat a mostly green color, but variegated with blue and gray tones

Lovecraftian terrifying in a monstrous or alien way; akin to the writing style of American writer H.P. Lovecraft

lovelock a lock of hair hanging separately

lowering dark and gloomy, as of threatening weather; scowling   **loxotic** distorted; slanted; lop-sided

lubricious smooth or slippery; wanton; salacious

luciferous illuminating, light-giving; figuratively, insightful

lucifugous shunning, avoiding or disliking light; nocturnal

lucriferous lucrative; profitable; economically advantageous

lucubration intense and prolonged study or meditation, esp. late at night; the product of such study, esp. written works

luculent lucid; clear; transparent, as luculent rivers; evident; luminous

Lucullan marked by lavishness & richness; sumptuous [after Roman general Lucullus, known for sumptuous banquets]

ludibund playful; sportive

ludic playful in a spontaneous or aimless manner; relating to play or playfulness

luftmensch an impractical dreamer having no real business or regular income [Yiddish (airman)]

lugubrious mournful, sad, or gloomy, esp. exaggeratedly so

lulu a remarkable person, idea, or thing

luminiferous bearing or bringing light

luminiferous aether in physics, the postulated medium for the propagation of light in the late 19th century

lumpen of a low, uneducated, boorish social class

lumpenproletariat the lowest, most degraded subclass of the proletariat

lunation lunar month **lunula** something crescent-shaped

lunisolar pertaining jointly to both the moon and the sun

lunulate shaped like a wee crescent

lupine of, like or pertaining to wolves

lurid gruesome; vivid and shocking; intensely fierce; ghastly glowing; wan

lustral of or pertaining to, or used for, purification; as, lustral days or lustral water; purifying **lustrate** to purify

lustrum period of five years; a lustration or purification, esp. the purification of the whole Roman people, which was made by the censors once in five years

luteous yellowish **lutescent** of a yellowish color

luxuria the deadly sin of lust; self-indulgent sexual longing

lycanthropy the supposed act of turning one's self or another into a wolf **lycanthropic**

lygophilia a preference for darkness

lygophilic a person who prefers or actively loves darkness (as opposed to **lygophobic**) [Greek lyge (twilight) + -philic]

lynx-eyed having acute eyesight

macarism a beatitude or blessing; making others happy through praise

macaronic characterized by a mixture of words from different languages

macilent lean, thin; of literary works, meager, thin or dry

macrobian long-lived

macromania delusion that objects, perhaps including one's own body, are larger than is natural

macropterous having large or long wings or fins

macroscian one casting a long shadow; inhabitant of high latitudes or polar regions [Greek macros (long) + skia (shadow)]

macrosmatic having a highly developed sense of smell

maculate to spot; to stain; marked with spots or maculae; defiled; impure **maculation** spots

madefy to make wet or moist

madescent becoming damp or moist **madid** wet or moist

maenad a female in Bacchanal or Dionysian rites; a frenzied woman **maenadic**

maggotorium a place where maggots are grown for fishing

magnality a great act or event; a great attainment

magnisonant high-sounding; bombastic; pretentious

mal du siècle world weariness
[French (sickness of the century)]

malar of or pertaining to the region of the cheek bone, or to the malar bone; jugal **malison** a curse; malediction

mallemaroking the carousing aboard icebound Greenland whaling ships

malloseismic an area likely to undergo several or more large earthquakes per century

malversation evil conduct; fraudulent practices; misbehavior, corruption, or extortion in office

mammer to hesitate or waiver; to mutter doubtfully

mammothrept literally, a child brought up by its grandmother; hence, a spoiled child [Greek mamma (grandmother)+ threptos (nourished, reared)]

mampara fool **manciple** a steward, esp. of a college

mandrel a spindle confining in the lathe the substance to be turned

mangonel a military engine formerly used for throwing stones and javelins

manikin a little man; a dwarf; a pygmy; a manikin

manqué one possessing the ability and potential for a particular job or achievement, but not having that ambition realized **manqueller** a killer of men; manslayer

mansuetude gentleness; meekness; mildness

mantic of, like or pertaining to divination; prophetic; inspired by a divine source

manticore in Persian & Greek mythology, a beast with a lion body, a scorpion tail, and a human head with rows of sharp teeth and the ability to shoot spikes from its tail to paralyze prey; may be horned or winged with a voice the mixture of pipes and trumpets   **mantilla** silk scarf

mantissa the decimal part of a logarithm

mantology fortune-telling

manumission freedom from slavery

manumit to release from slavery; to liberate from personal bondage or servitude; to free

manustupration masturbation

maquette a small model of an intended larger project, such as a sculptural or architectural work

maquillage makeup   **maquis** guerrilla resistance group

marcescent in botany, withering but not quite falling off; fading; decaying   **marcesible** likely to wither or fade

maremma a marshy seaside area, esp. in Italy

margent a margin or edge

marmoreal or **marmorean** like marble

marplot a meddling person who interferes in plans of others

marquetry inlaid work; work inlaid with pieces of wood, shells, or ivory of several colors

marquisette a sheer cotton fabric often used as mosquito netting or as curtains   **marsupium** marsupial pouch

massif in geology, the main mass of a mountain; a large fault block

Mata Hari a seductive woman working as a spy [from the stage name of a Dutch exotic dancer who spied for the Germans and the French executed in 1917 – Malay mata (eye) + hari (day, dawn), meaning sun]   **matelot** sailor

matripotestal of, like or pertaining to the powers of people who are mothers

maudlin tearfully or weakly sentimental in a foolish way, such as the inebriated sometimes act   **maunder** mutter

mawkish sentimental in a weak, insincere or exaggerated way

Maxwellian of or relating to shady business practices, financial tricks, embezzlement, etc.

maya the illusory appearance of the material world as known to the senses [Sanskrit]

mazard the jaw; the head or skull

mazarine a deep, rich blue color   **mazel** luck [Yiddish]

mazy perplexed with turns and windings; intricate or convoluted; perplexing   **meable** penetrable with ease

mechanomorphism belief that the universe behaves like a machine **mechanomorphic**

mediagenic presenting an attractive image in the media

medusiform resembling a jellyfish in shape or structure

meed that which is rewarded for merit; just recompense

meeken to make more meek, to nurture in gentleness and/or humility   **megascopic** perceptible to unaided eyesight

megrim migraine; low spirits or depression; a whim or fancy

melange a mixture

melic of or pertaining to song; lyric; tuneful

meliphagous honey-eating, feeding on honey or nectar

melisma (pl. **melismata**) a piece of melody, song or tune **melismatic**

melliferous producing honey

mellifluence a flow of sweetness; a smooth, honeyed flow

mellifluent or **mellifluous** smooth-flowing; sweet-sounding

melliloquent sweet and harmonious in speech

mellisonant sweet-sounding   **mellisugent** honey-sucking

melomania an extreme passion for music

menarche a human female's first menstrual period

mentation process of careful thought or consideration

mephitic of or resembling mephitis; poisonous; noxious; offensive-smelling

mephitis a foul exhalation from decomposing substances or other sources; a stench

meracious pure; without adulteration; unmixed

mercer a dealer in textile fabrics

meretricious seemingly plausible, but false; superficially attractive; specious

merry-andrew a buffoon; one who amuses people by

clowning around **meseems** it seems to me

meshuga crazy; stupid or foolish [Yiddish meshuge]

mesonoxian of or pertaining to midnight

metachrosis in biology, the ability of animals to change color

metagrobolism concealment; mystification; obfuscation

metagrobolized totally mixed up or confused

metempirics concepts deemed beyond, but related to, experiential knowledge

metempsychosis the transmission of a soul from one dying body into another living one

methomania an irresistible craving for alcohol

metic a sojourner; an immigrant; an alien resident in a Grecian city

metrics the art of versification or of using poetical meter

metromania a mania for writing verse

mickle or **meikle** large, great; much, many

mien carriage; bearing; appearance; countenance

millenarianism belief that Christ will reign on Earth for a thousand years; a Chiliast

millesimal a thousandth; consisting of a thousand parts

milliad period of a thousand years **milliard** a billion

mim prim; demure **mimbar** a mosque's pulpit

mimetic imitative; apt to imitate

minify to diminish; to lessen; to degrade by speech or action

minimifidian having the tiniest amount of faith

mirabilia wonders

mirabiliary having to do with miracle working

mirador a window with a good view

mirific working wonders; wonderful

misaunter misadventure

misbeseem to be not well suited for

miscible capable of being mixed together; mixable

mise en abyme self-reflection or introspection in a literary or other artistic work; the representation of the whole work embedded in a work

mislight to lead astray by a false light

misoneism hatred of change

misprize to slight or undervalue

mistral strong and cold Mediterranean wind

misyoke to yoke improperly; to marry unsuitably

mithridate poison antidote

mizmaze labyrinth or maze; bewilderment

mizzle to rain in very fine drops

mnesic pertaining to memory

moanworthy worthy of sorrowful moaning; worthy of lament

mobocracy government by mobs or crowds

modish according to fashion; stylish   **moil** to toil

moilsome laborious   **mokita** the truth that is known by everyone but talked about by no one

molder to decay or crumble; to disintegrate

moliminous of great bulk or consequence; very important [Latin molimen (effort, weight, importance)]

mollescent softening   **mollipilose** downy; soft; having soft hairs or plumage   **monachal** monastic

monadnock a hill or mountain standing isolated, having resisted erosion, above a plain

mondegreen slip of the ear; the mishearing of something

mononymous someone having or being known by only one name, e.g. Plato

monopsychism doctrine that there is only one immortal soul, with which all people are endowed

monotroch wheelbarrow   **montgolfier** a hot-air balloon

monticle a little mount; a hillock

monticolous mountain-dwelling

montivagant wandering over mountains

moonblink a temporary blindness, or impairment of sight, said to be caused by sleeping in the moonlight

mooncalf a fool, monster or freak; the issuance of a false conception

moon-eyed having eyes wide open in sorrow, infatuation, or wonder; purblind

moonglade the bright reflection of the moon's light on an expanse of water

moon-splashed something covered by patches of moonlight

morassic of, like or pertaining to a morass

morbidezza in art, delicacy or softness in the representation of flesh; in music, to execute with extreme delicacy

moria folly; idiocy; imbecility; fatuity; foolishness

morosoph a fool who has been formally educated or is prone to philosophical musings

morphallaxis regeneration of specific tissue after loss of same, as a lobster claw

morphean of or relating to Morpheus, to dreams, or to sleep

morpheme the smallest unit of meaning in a language

morro rounded hill or headland; esp. one with a castle atop

mortmain the perpetual, inalienable possession of lands by a corporation or non-personal entity such as a church

mosstrooper a marauder (from the bandits that tromped the moorland between England and Scotland in olden times)

mother out-law the mother of an ex-wife or ex-husband (in contradistinction to mother in-law)

motrix a female instigator or cause of something

mouchard a police-spy, esp. in a Francophone country

moue (mü) a little grimace; a pout, esp. as expressing mock annoyance or flirtatiousness

moulin a vertical shaft in a glacier carved out by meltwater

mountebank a traveling quack who attracts customers with stories or tricks; a charlatan

moxie bravery; determination; energy; skill

mucid moldy; musty; slimy; mucous

muciferous conveying or secreting mucus

mucilage a sticky substance secreted by some plants; any sticky substance used as adhesive

muciparous or **mucigenous** producing or secreting mucus

muckender handkerchief

mucopurulent having the character or appearance of both mucus & pus

muculent slimy, moist, and moderately viscous; like mucus

mudlark one who scavenges in river mud for valuable items

mugwump one who is politically independent or neutral

muliebrity the state of being a woman or of possessing full womanly powers; womanhood; a correlate of virility; effeminacy; softness **muliebral**

multeity multiplicity [from Latin multus (much, many)]

multiloculate possessing many small cavities or cells

multiloquent talkative; garrulous; loquacious

mumblecrust toothless beggar

mummery any display, parade or ceremony that is pretentious or hypocritical; a farcical show

mumpsimus a view stubbornly clung to even after shown to be wrong; one holding such a view [from an historical blunder for Latin sumpsimus (we have received)]

mundivagant wandering around the world

murmuration the act of murmuring; a murmur; (of starlings) a flock

murmurous murmuring; exciting murmurs or complaint

murrey a dark red or mulberry color

musal of or pertaining to the Muses, or to poetry

musard a dreamer; an absent-minded person

musical texture the way the melodic, rhythmic, and harmonic elements are combined in a composition

Muspelheim one of the nine worlds in Norse mythology, full of fire, light and heat

mussitate to mumble; to mutter

multanimous possessing a many-sided mind

muzzy absent-minded; dazed; muddled

myrmidon a loyal follower, esp. a soldier or a subordinate civil officer who executes orders (esp. cruel orders) of a superior without protest or pity [from members of the warrior nation of ancient Thessaly, Greece, that were led by Achilles in the Trojan War]

mystagogical or **mystagogic** of or pertaining to interpretation of mysteries or to a mystagogue

mystagogue a person who prepares an initiate for entry into a secret cult, or who teaches mystical doctrines

mythoclast a destroyer of myths

mythogenesis the creation of myths; the ability or tendency to originate myths

mythologem a basic and universal mythic theme, such as revenge, honor, or betrayal

mythomania an abnormal compulsion to tell lies or to exaggerate **mythomaniac**

mythopoeia or **mythopoesis** the creation of any myth

mythopoeic giving rise to myths; pertaining to the creation of myth

nacarat a pale red color, with a cast of orange

nacreous having a pearly luster; resembling mother-of-pearl

naif one who is naive

naissant nascent; newly born; in heraldry, same as jessant: springing up or emerging

nanization artificial dwarfing of trees, esp. as practiced by the Japanese **nanocephalous** having a very small head

naos or **cella** that part of an ancient temple enclosed by walls

narcokleptocracy rule by drug lords

narcotized in some way under the influence of narcotics

narquois mocking; malicious **nates** the buttocks

natheless nevertheless; notwithstanding

nativism in philosophy, the doctrine that the mind possesses forms of thought independent of sensation

natricine of, like or pertaining to the genus of serpent which includes grass snakes and watersnakes

naufragous causing shipwreck

naumachia a naval battle; esp., a mock sea fight put on by the ancient Romans **naze** a promontory or headland

neanic of, like or pertaining to youth, the adolescent period, or the early stages; young

neanimorphic appearing younger than one's actual age [Greek neanikos (youthful)]

neaped or **beneaped** left aground, as boats grounded by tide

nebris the fawn-skin worn by Dionysus and his followers

[Greek mythology]

nebulize to reduce (as a liquid) to a fine spray or vapor; to atomize

nebulochaotic a hazy, confused or chaotic state of mind

nebulose or **nebulous** cloudy; foggy; not possessing a definite form

necessarium a lavatory; a toilet, esp. in a monastery

necromancy the art of revealing future events by means of communication with the dead; magic in general; conjuration; enchantment

necromimesis falsely believing oneself to be dead; pretending to be dead   **nemophila** a genus of flower

nemophilist one who is fond of forest or forest scenery; a haunter of the woods

nemoral of or pertaining to a wood or grove

nemorous woodsy; treed

neoblastic pertaining to new growth or new tissue

neoteric modern, recent, newfangled

nepenthe (ni-PEN-thee) something, esp. a drink, that causes one to forget their troubles or their suffering [from a drug mentioned in the Odyssey as a remedy for grief]

nephalism total abstinence from spirituous liquor or alcohol of any sort   **nepheliad** a cloud nymph

nepheligenous discharging clouds of smoke, esp. of tobacco

nephelosphere cloudy envelope surrounding a planet

nephogram a photograph of clouds

nephophobia a fear of clouds

nescience the absence of knowledge; ignorance

nescient ignorant person; an unbeliever; unlearned

nesh soft; delicate; tender   **nesiote** inhabiting an island

nestcock a househusband; a delicate man who stays at home

nevus or **naevus** (pl. **nevi**) birthmark

nidorosity belching with the taste of undigested meat

Niflheim one of the nine worlds in Norse mythology, with nine frozen rivers, mists, and cold lands

night-foundered lost and in distress during the night

night soil human feces used as fertilizer

nigrescence becoming black or dark; a dark complexion

nihilarian a person who deals with things lacking importance

nikhedonia the pleasure one feels anticipating success

nimbose cloudy; stormy; tempestuous

nimbus (pl. **nimbi** or **nimbuses**) a rain cloud; in classic art, a disk of radiant light around the heads of divinities, saints, and sovereigns [Latin nimbus (cloud)]

ninnyhammer a simpleton; a silly person

nival relating to snow; abounding with snow; snowy

niveous snowy; resembling snow

nobilitate to make noble; to ennoble; to exalt

nocebo a harmless substance which a patient experiences as harmful merely because he or she believes it to be harmful

noctiflorous flowering by night

noctilucent glowing in the dark or at night

noctilucous shining by night; luminescent

noctivagant roving or wandering at night

noctuary a record of what passes in the night; a nightly journal

nod-crafty nodding with great wisdom

nodus a knot in rope or wood; a sticking point or complication

noesis intellectual activity; cognition; the use of reason; intellectual, not sensory, perception

noetic of or pertaining to the mind or intellect; originating in or apprehended by reason

noetics the branch of metaphysical philosophy concerning the study of mind and intellect

nolens volens whether willing or unwilling; willy-nilly

nomancy the art of divining a person's destiny using the letters of his or her name

nomothetic relating to law-making; legislative

nonesuch paragon; an extraordinary thing; a thing that has no equal

nonpareil something of unequaled excellence; a peerless thing or person; a nonesuch

nonplus to puzzle; to confound; to perplex

noogenesis the emergence of intelligent forms of life

noosphere sphere of human thought; a theoretical stage of evolutionary development, associated with consciousness, the mind, and personal relationships (often with reference to the writings of Teilhard de Chardin)

nootropics drugs that enhance learning and memory

nosism the practice of using the pronoun "we" to refer to oneself, including the royal we and the editorial we

nostomania an overwhelming desire to return to familiar surroundings, or to one's home

nostrum a medicine that has no proven positive medicinal benefit; hypothetical panacea

notandum a thing to be noted or observed; a notable fact

nothingarian one of no certain belief; one belonging to no particular religion

noumenon (pl. **noumena**) a thing in itself; a thing which can be assumed to exist by reason or intuition as opposed to phenomenon which is apprehended by the senses

nous intellect; understanding

novena in Catholicism, a nine-day period of special prayer

nubecula a nebula or nebulae, esp. one of the Magellanic Clouds   **nubiferous** bringing, or producing, clouds

nubigenous born of, or produced from, clouds

nubilate to obscure or cloud

nubilous cloudy, misty, or foggy; overcast; not clear

nubivagant wandering in the clouds; moving thru the air

nullibiety the state of being nowhere

nullipara or **nullip** (nah-LIP-er-ah) refers to a woman who has never given birth

numen (pl. **numina**) a divinity, esp. a local or presiding god; creative energy

numinous relating to a numen; indicating the presence of a divinity; awe-inspiring; evoking a sense of the transcendent, mystical or sublime; supernatural, mysterious; spiritual; appealing to lofty emotions or aesthetic sense   **nummamorous** fond of money

nutant nodding; drooping; having the top bent downward

nyctanthous in botany, having flowers that open at night

nycthemeron the natural day and night; the space of twenty-four hours   **nyctophilia** preferring the night or darkness

nymphaeum ancient shrine, often with a fountain, that was dedicated to water nymphs

nympholepsy a demoniac enthusiasm or possession arising from seeing a nymph; ecstasy; a frenzied emotional (and usually erotic) state, esp. arising from a desire for something or someone unattainable

obambulate to walk about; to wander without purpose

obelus (pl. **obeli**) the symbol mostly used to represent division in math

oblectation the act of pleasing highly; the state of being greatly pleased; delight

obliquation obliqueness; declination from a strait line; a turning to one side; deviation from moral rectitude

obliquitous deviating from good morals or from logical thinking

obliquity the state or quality of being oblique; an oblique statement or action

oblivescence forgetfulness; forgetting

obmutescent speechless; habitually silent; preferring silence

obnubilate cloudy, foggy; to becloud; to obscure [Latin ob (in the way) + nubilus (cloudy)]

obsolagnium the lessening of sexual desire in old age

obtenebrate to darken; to enshadow something

obtest to beg, beseech or implore

obumbrate to cast a shadow upon; to shade; to darken

obvallate walled in (esp. in botany)

obvelation a concealing; opposite of revelation

obverse the front side of something, like heads on a coin

obvolute overlapping; contorted; convoluted

ocellus a little eye; a simple eye found in invertebrates;

an eye-like spot of color, as on a peacock's tail

ochlocracy (aw-kl-ah-kreh-see) a form of government by the multitude; a mobocracy; government by the common people **ochlophobia** obsessive fear of mob-like crowds

ochreous or **ocherous** consisting of or resembling ocher; ocherous, or yellowish, in color

octothorp(e) the # symbol, as on telephone pads and keyboards (hash, pound sign, number sign)

oculus an eye; a round window, usually a small one and esp. above the door to a church

od in physics, an alleged force or natural power, historically supposed by some to produce the phenomena of mesmerism, and to be developed by various agencies including magnets, heat, light, chemical action, etc.

odalisque a female slave or concubine in a harem, esp. in that of a Turkish sultan

odditorium a museum or other place where oddities are on display

Odic force name given in the mid-19th century to a hypothetical vital energy or life force by Baron Carl von Reichenbach

oddment something left over; something unusual

oeillade a glance or wink, esp. an amorous one; an ogle

oenomel a beverage comprised of wine and honey

oeuvre the complete body of an artist's work

offing far enough offshore so that deep water obviates the need for a marine pilot; distance from the shore; the distance a ship keeps from land, often because of navigational dangers; figuratively, the foreseeable future (usually "in the offing")

okta in meteorology, one eighth of the area of the sky (the celestial dome); used as a measure of cloudiness (six oktas means that 3/4 of the sky is obscured, for example)

olamic of or pertaining to a very long time period; everlasting, eternal [Hebrew olam (eternity)]

olfactible having an odor; capable of being smelled

olid foul-smelling

oligomania an obsession, neurosis, or psychosis that is only evident in a few directions of thought, or in relation to a few themes or ideas

ololygmancy fortune telling by listening to canine howling

ombibulous someone, or something, that drinks anything

ombrophilous tolerant of wet conditions or of heavy rainfall; rain-loving **ombrophobia** fear of rain

omneity everything existent; that which understands everything; allness; state of being all

omniana pieces of information touching on a wide variety of subjects **omniferous** producing all kinds

omnific or **omnificent** capable of making or doing anything; all-creating **omnify** to enlarge; to render universal

omnigenous consisting of all kinds

omnilegent extremely well-read; having read everything; having expansive knowledge

omninescience completely ignorant; having knowledge of nothing at all

omnishambles several shambles (big messes) grouped together by time, place, cause, etc.

omnigatherum or **omnium-gatherum** a miscellaneous assortment of things; hodgepodge

omnivagant wandering everywhere

omphalos the navel; a boss; a centerpiece

oneiric dreamy; of or relating to dreams

oneirodynia nightmare or bad dreams

oneiromancy the art of predicting the future by interpreting dreams **oneiromancer**

onomastic of, or relating to a personal or place name

ontic whatever pertains to actual being, rather than some theory of it **oofy** wealthy, rich

oolert or **owlerd** the barn owl (provincial English usage)

opacular opaque or nearly opaque

opalescence a reflection of a milky or pearly light from the interior of a mineral, as in the moonstone; the state or quality of being opalescent

ophidian of, like, or pertaining to snakes or serpents

ophiolatry snake-worship

opsimath one who begins (or continues) a marked path of learning (or study) late in life

optative expressing desire or wish; in grammar, the form of a verb in which wish or desire is expressed

opusculum a short literary work

oragious stormy   **orbific** world-making

orchidaceous of or pertaining to orchids; characterized by ostentation; showy

orchidectomy surgical procedure to remove one or both testes; castration   **oread** a mountain nymph

orectic of or pertaining to the desires; impelling to gratification; appetitive

orenda a mystical, spiritual energy or power believed by traditional Iroquois to pervade all things in nature

orexis (pl. **orexes**) in psychology, the emotional or purposeful character of mental activity as contrasted with its cognitive aspect; the appetitive aspect of an act; desire, appetite

orison a prayer; "And, as Echo far off through the vale my sad orison rolls / I think, oh, my love! 'tis thy voice from the Kingdom of Souls" – Thomas Moore

orogen a belt of mountains created by orogenesis

orogenesis mountain-building geological processes

orpharion or **orpheoreon** a Renaissance stringed musical instrument, similar to the lute

orphic like Orpheus, the ancient Greek poet and musician; mystic or occult; entrancing

orphrey a band of rich embroidery, wholly or in part of gold, affixed to vestments

orthopraxis correct conduct in religion

oscitant yawning; sleepy; drowsy; dull; sluggish

osculate to kiss   **osmesis** the sense of smell; act of smelling

osmidrosis secretion of ill-smelling sweat

ostracon an inscribed potsherd

ostrichism policy of ignoring the reality of unpleasant facts

ostrobogulous slightly risqué or indecent; bizarre; interesting; unusual **ostrobogulatory**

otacust spy; scout; eavesdropper

otic of, like, or pertaining to, or in the region of, the ear; auricular; auditory

oubliette a dungeon with a door in the ceiling only

ouphe a fairy, goblin or elf

ouroboros a serpent or dragon who eats its own tail, representing the cycle of life and death, totality, or completion; a picture or symbol depicting this

outfling a gibe; a contemptuous remark

outjet that which projects from something

outmantle to excel in mantling; to excel in splendor, dress or ornament; "She outmantles a setting sun, out-glistens crepuscular moons." **outpassion** to exceed in passion

outrance the utmost or last extremity; the bitter end

outré or **outre** unconventional or bizarre; beyond what is considered normal

outremer area beyond the sea; overseas; ultramarine; a brilliant pure dark blue or slightly purplish color [French outre-mer ("beyond the sea")]

outrider an escort, esp. one who rides in advance; a forerunner   **overfall** waterfall; undersea drop off

overflush to flush to excess

overmorrow the day after tomorrow

overween to think arrogantly; to regard one's own thinking too highly; to presume

overweening unduly confident; arrogant; presumptuous; conceited

ovine pertaining to sheep; sheep-like   **oxter** armpit; axilla

ozostomia foul breath; halitosis

pabulous of, like or pertaining to nourishment or food

pabulum food; provender; nourishment; aliment

pactolian like or having golden sands [from Pactolus, a river in ancient Lydia famous for its golden-hued sands]

paillette a spangle or sequin

palabra a word; speech or talk; palaver

paladin a knight-errant; a distinguished or heroic champion; an ardent supporter of a cause

palatine of or relating to powers normally possessed by a sovereign but exercised by a lesser noble, or by a nominee of a sovereign; of or relating to a palace

palatium a palace or very large residence

palaverous wordy; verbose

paleomnesia a good memory of happenings of the long ago past **palestrian** pertaining to wrestling

palimpsest a manuscript or document that has been erased for reuse of the paper

palingenesis spiritual rebirth through the transmigration of the soul in Christian baptism **palingenetic**

palisade a wall of wooden stakes, used as a defensive barrier; a line of cliffs, esp. along a river

palladian pertaining to wisdom or learning; in Greek mythology, of or related to Athena

palladium that which affords effectual protection or security; a safeguard

palliate to ameliorate; to hide or disguise; to hide the seriousness of a mistake; to placate or mollify; to mitigate [Latin pallium (cloak)] **palmy** flourishing, prosperous

palp in zoology, a sensory appendage found near the mouth in invertebrates; the fleshy part of a fingertip; to feel, to explore by touch **palpebra** eyelid **palpebral**

palsa a small dome-shaped frost mound 10 to 20 feet in height, containing peat

paludal of or pertaining to marshes or fens; marshy

panarchy universal rule; in diplomacy, an inclusive, multilaterial system in which all parties may participate meaningfully; an all-encompassing realm **panarchic**

pandiculation a stretching and stiffening of the trunk and extremities, as when fatigued and drowsy or on waking, often accompanied by yawning

Panglossian overly optimistic [after Dr Pangloss, a character in Voltaire's Candide]   **panharmonic** in universal accord

panoptic seeing everything or all things at once; including everything visible in one view

panspermia the theory that microorganisms or biochemical compounds from interstellar space cause life to originate on Earth and perhaps in other parts of the galaxy and universe where life-supporting conditions exist

Pantagruelian gigantic; voracious; insatiable; utilizing excessive and vulgar satiric humor [after Pantagruel, a giant king with an huge appetite, featured in a series of novels by François Rabelais]

panmixia or **panmixis** random mating within a given population, with no physical, genetic, or social preference **panmictic**

pantalets or **pantalettes** a form of long underpants with a frill at the bottom of each leg

pantisocracy a Utopian community in which all rule equally

pantograph an instrument for copying plans, maps, and other drawings on the same or on a larger or smaller scale

pantomorphic capable of assuming any form or shape

pantoscopic literally, seeing everything; applied to bifocal eyeglasses and to wide-angle photography

panurgic skilled in all kinds of work

Paphian pertaining to Paphos, birthplace of Aphrodite, the goddess of love, on Cyprus; relating to love or sexual yearnings, esp. when unlawful

papilionaceous resembling, or pertaining to, the butterfly

paracme a point beyond the highest or past the prime [Greek parakma (to be past the prime)]

paradromic adjacent; running side by side; parallel

paralian a person who dwells near the sea

paramnesia a misremembering of events by confusing actual memories with dreams or fantasies

paramo a treeless grassland ecosystem covering extensive high areas of equatorial mountains, esp. in South America

paranymph a bridesmaid or brideman; one who leads the bride to her marriage; a bestman; one who countenances and supports another; an ally

paraph a flourish made with the pen at the end of a signature [used in the Middle Ages as a safeguard against forgery]

parapraxis a mistake, such as a slip of the tongue, that reveals a concealed thought or motive

parapsychic relating to paranormal mental phenomenon for which there are no scientific explanations, such as telepathy, psychokinesis, etc.

parasang an ancient Persian measure of distance estimated at about 5.6 kilometers

paraselene mock moon; a bright patch on a lunar halo

paravent a screen for blocking the wind   **parbreak** to vomit

parfay by my faith; verily

parhelion sundog; a mock sun, appearing as a bright, sometimes rainbow-like, light near the sun

parisology the deliberate use of ambiguity in language

parlous dangerous; venturesome; bold

Parnassian of or pertaining to poetry, or the Muses

parquetry the technique of applying wooden tiles or veneers to create a decorative geometrical pattern on floors, furniture, etc.

parterre formal flower garden, often forming a pattern; an apartment or theater balcony

parthenian of, like, or pertaining to virgins

parthenogenesis in some plant and insect species, generation without fertilization; asexual reproduction; virgin birth, conception without sex [Greek parthenos (virgin) + genesis (beginning, birth)]

parthian shot a hostile, departing remark [Parthians were archers known for firing arrows whilst in retreat (or pretending to retreat)]

parvanimity having a small or ignoble mind; pettiness (opposite of magnanimity)

parvenu (feminine form: **parvenue**) one who has suddenly risen to a monied or powerful life-position and has not yet acquired the manner commonly associated with that position

pasigraphy a system of symbolic language that can be universally understood

pasquinade to satirize or lampoon **pasquilant** lampooner

passel a indeterminately large number or group

passerine of or relating to the largest order of birds, Passeres, comprised mostly of perching songbirds such as sparrows

passible susceptible of feeling or suffering, or of impressions from external agents **passim** here and there; everywhere

patagium fold of skin in bats or flying squirrels that connects from body to forelimb and forms a wing-like extension

pataphysics the pseudo-scientific or philosophical study of imaginary phenomena that may exist beyond metaphysics; the science of imaginary solutions [from French writer Alfred Jarry, 1873–1907]

pathos passion; contagious warmth or vehemence in speech; in language, that which excites emotions and passions, esp. emotions such as pity and sorrow

patrial of, like or pertaining to one's country of origin

patulous in botany, spreading or expanded; open; exposed; having loose or dispersed parts **pavid** timid; fearful

pavis a medieval shield large offering full body protection

pavonine characteristic of a peacock, esp. its colorful tail; iridescent **paysage** countryside; landscape

pecksniffian selfish and corrupt behind a benevolent display; sanctimonious **pediment** gable

pelagic of the ocean surface or the open sea

pelf money or riches, esp. if ill-gotten

pellicle a thin skin, such as the skin of a mushroom cap; a thin film

pellucid perfectly clear; transparent; limpid; translucent

pelma sole of foot **pelmatogram** footprint, esp. taken as an imprint on paper or in plaster

pendragon a chief or dictator; title bequeathed on a chief of chiefs in ancient Britain

pendulate to swing as a pendulum; fluctuate, undulate

penelopize from Greek myth., to act like Odysseus' wife Penelope and undo work then start it again to gain time

penetralia the innermost recesses of any thing or place, esp. of a temple or palace; hidden things or secrets; sanctuary

peneplain a nearly flat plain formed by a long period of fluvial erosion

pennaceous like or pertaining to a normal feather

pentalpha pentangle; pentacle; pentagram; five-pointed star

pentapolis any group of five cities, esp. ones that are allied

penumbra a partial shadow, as in the margin of an eclipse; anywhere something exists to a lesser degree; any outlying and surrounding area

peradventure by chance; perhaps; it may be; if; supposing

peragrate to travel over or through

percipient having the faculty of perception; particularly discerning

percurrent running throughout; in biology, running the whole length

perdu one placed on watch, or in an ambush; concealed; lost

perdurable very durable; permanent; everlasting

perfervid very fervid; ardent; impassioned

perforce by necessity; in a way that cannot be avoided

perfuse to permeate or suffuse something with liquid or light

pergamenous resembling parchment

peri a fairy in Persian mythology; a beautiful, graceful female

periblepsis the wild gaze that may accompany delirium

periclinal sloping down on every side from a single point

periclitate to endanger

perijove point at which any Jovian satellite comes closest to Jupiter

periplus a circumnavigation; an epic voyage around a sea or a land; an account of such a voyage

periscian person whose shadow circumvolves through the day; someone living inside the polar circle

perissological redundant in word usage; using more words than necessary or appropriate

peristrephic turning around, revolving, rotating

peritectic in an intermediate phase of matter between solid and liquid **periwinkle** bluish or azure color

perlaceous pearly; resembling pearl

perlustrate to travel through and examine an area; to survey thoroughly

pernoctation the act of staying out all night or remaining somewhere all night

perpend ponder; to weight carefully in the mind

perse dark purplish black color

perseity having an independent state of being

persiflage a light, frivolous or flippant style of writing or speaking; such talk or writing

persiflate to talk in a bantering way

persifleur one who banters, or engages in persiflage

personalia all the personal allusions, belongings,writings, information, of an individual

perstringe to criticize; to imply; to glance on

perulate in botany, scaly

pessimal bad to a maximal extent; worst; of an organism's environment, least conducive to survival **pessimum**

petrichor the distinctive scent of first rain after a dry spell; any post-rain smell of earth [Greek petra (rock) + ichor (blood of the gods)]

petricolous rock-dwelling; living among or on rocks

petronel a 17th century firearm

petrous like stone; hard; stony; rocky

pettifogger a lawyer who deals in petty cases; an attorney with dishonest or shady methods

phalacrosis baldness **phallocracy** government by men

phallocratic pertaining to government or dominance by males **phallocrat**

phantasmagoria an 18th- and 19th-century form of theater entertainment whereby ghostly apparitions are formed; a magic lantern; a series of events involving rapid changes in light intensity and color; a dreamlike state where real and imagined elements are blurred together

pharos any lighthouse for nautical guidance; a watch-tower; a beacon   **phasmophobia** a fear of ghosts

phatic pertaining to words used for social reasons or to communicate feelings rather than for meaning; for example, "How are you?" is often not a literal question, but only a greeting

phellem cork   **philalethist** a lover of the truth

philia friendly love; friendship; liking

Philippic any discourse or declamation abounding in acrimonious invective

phillumenist a collector of matchbooks

philocalist one who loves beauty

philodox a person who loves his or her own opinions; stubbornly opinionated

philomuse a lover of poetry, literature, and the arts

philopolemic ruling over opposite or contending natures; disputatious, as someone who loves to debate

philtrum the vertical shallow groove running from the nose down the center of the upper lip

Phlegethon a river in Hades, flowing with fire instead of water [Greek mythology]

phlegmatic not easily excited to action or passion; cold; dull; sluggish; apathetic

Phoebus another name of Apollo, God of the sun; the sun

photic of or related to light, esp. relating to the production of light by the lower animals; light-giving, sensitive to light

photism in psychology, a luminous image or appearance of a hallucinatory character   **photogyric** turning towards light

phrenesis delirium or frenzy

phrontifugic helping to escape from or ease anxiety

phrontistery a school or seminary of learning; a place for study or thought

phthartic deadly, destructive [Greek phthartikos (destructive)]

phylon a tribe

physis nature as the power behind growth or change; something that grows or changes

piacular expiatory; atoning

picaresque like a rascal, rogue or adventurer

picaroon or **picaro** one who plunders, esp. a plunderer of wrecks; a pirate; a corsair; a marauder

picksome particular; picky

pierian having to do with poetry, the arts or artistic inspiration; "A little learning is a dang'rous thing; Drink deep, or taste not the Pierian spring." – Pope [in Greek mythology the Pierian Spring of Macedonia was sacred to the Muses]

pieties pious actions, statements, thoughts, or beliefs

pigmentocracy government by those of the same skin color

pilcrow a paragraph mark; ¶   **pileus** mushroom cap

piloerection hairs standing on end

pilliwinks a medieval instrument of torture designed to slowly crush the fingers or thumbs

pillock a person somewhat lacking intelligence

pinchbeck an alloy of copper and zinc, used to imitate gold; sham; cheap; unreal

piolet ice axe used by mountain climbers

piquerism or **picquerism** sexual interest in penetrating someone's skin, sometimes to the point of death [French piquer (to prick)]

pisher a bedwetter; an inexperienced or insignificant person

pithead the area around the top of a coal mine's mineshaft, usually including the entrance

pixilated mentally unbalanced; eccentric; whimsical [from pixie, a mischievous fairy-like creature]

pizzle an animal's penis, esp. the bull cow; a bull's penis historically made into a whip

placentious pleasing; amiable   **plangent** having a loud, mournful sound   **plangorous** mournful

plapper to make a noise with the lips

plash a puddle; a dash of water

plashy watery; full of puddles or pools; splashy

plastron breastplate; padded leather worn by fencers; front panel of a dress shirt or tunic

pleach to unite by interweaving, as branches of trees; to plash; to interlock; to interlace; to braid; "the pleached bower"   **pleasance** a secluded part of a garden

plebification to render plebeian; to vulgarize

plectile woven or plaited

plectrum a pick for a guitar, lyre, or other stringed instrument

plenilunary of or pertaining to the full moon

pleochroic showing different colors when viewed from different directions, as some crystals

pleonasm redundancy of language in speaking or writing

pleroma a state of perfect fullness, esp. of God's being

plexure network or that which is woven together; the act or process of weaving together, or interweaving

plication a folding or fold   **plighted** promised or bound by a solemn pledge, esp. betrothed

plodge walking through mud or mire   **pluck** spirit; courage; indomitable resolution; fortitude

plumbless incapable of being measured or sounded; unfathomable

plumigerous feathered; plumaged; wearing feathers

plumulate minutely plumose; downy

pluripresence presence in more than one place

plushy sumptuous; plush; luxurious; soft and shaggy

pluterperfect more than perfect; "The pluterperfect imperturbability of the department of agriculture" – James Joyce, Ulysses

pluto to demote or devalue someone or something [as happened to the former planet Pluto]

plutomania a passion or craving for wealth; an obsession with money; the delusion that one is wealthy

plutonic igneous; subject to the influence of volcanic heat or subterranean pressures; pertaining to Pluto; Plutonian;

pertaining to the interior of the earth; subterranean

pluviophile someone who loves the rain

pneuma the soul; the living spirit; breathe

poindexter a bookish or socially unskilled person

politesse exceptional civility, politeness, courtesy or gallantry, or an instance of this   **politicaster** a petty politician

pollard a tree pruned by cutting branches close to the trunk to promote more bushy growth; an animal, such as cattle or deer, whose horns have been removed or shed

pollent strong

pollex the first digit of the fore limb; the thumb

polyergic having multiple functions, or functioning in different ways

polymythy the use of several plots in one narrative

polyphiloprogenitive extremely prolific, fertile, or imaginative

polysemous having many different meanings, such as some words

pomosexual perhaps similar to being nonpartisan in politics, non-orientated sexually, not adhering or identifying oneself or others by labels such as gay, straight, etc.

pontlevis a drawbridge; the action of a horse rearing repeatedly and dangerously

pooh-pooh to make light of; to treat with derision or contempt   **porphyrous** purple

portcullis an iron grate used as a gate in a castle or fortress

postlapsarian pertaining to anything which follows a lapse or failure; in Christianity, the state of being which followed the expulsion of Adam and Eve from the Garden of Eden

postmundane after the end of the world

postulant a candidate for something, esp. for entrance to a religious order   **potatory** of or pertaining to drinking

pot-valiant or **potvaliant** exhibiting bravado as a result of being drunk   **pourparler** pre-treaty discussions

prairillon a small meadow, prairie, or stretch of grassland

prajna wisdom or understanding [Buddhism]

pranava the meditative word "om", commonly used as a mantra [Hinduism]

prandial of or pertaining to a meal, esp. dinner

pratal growing in meadows

prate prattle; chatter; babble; idle, foolish talk

pratfall a fall upon one's arse; figuratively, a embarrassing mistake

praxis practice, esp. exercise or discipline for a specific purpose; practical application or exercise of an area of learning; established practice   **preadamic** prior to Adam

preantepenultimate fourth from the last [from Latin pre- (before) + ante- (before) + pen- (almost) + ultimus (last)]

precentor a leader of a choir; a directing singer

predacious predatory; living by or characterized by robbing or exploiting others, or by taking prey

predicate to found; to base   **prefatory** pertaining to a preface; introductory to a book, essay or discourse

prefulgent brighter, or more fulgent, than others

pregustation the act of tasting beforehand; foretaste

prelapsarian relating to before the Fall; Eden before the lost innocence of Adam and Eve; relating to any past period of carefree innocence [from Latin pre (before) + lapsus (fall)]

prelusive of the nature of a prelude; introductory; indicating that something of a like kind is to follow

premonish to forewarn; to admonish beforehand

preponderate to outweigh; to overpower by weight; to exceed in weight

prepone to reschedule an event to a time earlier than the originally scheduled time

prepossessing immediately impressing favorably; attracting confidence, favor, esteem, or love; attractive, as a prepossessing manner

presque vu a feeling that you are on the edge of grasping something; having something on the "tip of your tongue" [French (nearly seen)]

preta hungry ghosts that, due to bad karma (greed, etc.) in a previous life, return with an insatiable hunger for something, often feces or corpses [Hindu & Buddhist lore]

preterhuman more than human; beyond what is commonly characteristic of a human

preterist one who regards the past with great pleasure or favor **preterlapsed** past, as preterlapsed centuries

pretermission intentionally overlooking or disregarding something

preternatural beyond normal; supernatural

pretervection the act of carrying past or beyond

prevaricate to stray from a direct course, esp. to stray from the truth; equivocate

prevenancy politely anticipating another person's wishes

prevernal occurring just before the leafing of any trees; blossoming or foliating early

prevision foresight; foreknowledge

prevoyant foreseeing; prescient

pridian of or pertaining to yesterday

princesse lointaine an ideal but unattainable female love interest [French (distant princess)]

prink to dress or adjust one's self for show **prinker**

procellous stormy [Latin procella (storm)]

proclivitous or **proclivous** sloping steeply

procreant generating; producing; fruitful; assisting in procreation

Procrustes a legendary Attican highwayman who tied victims to an iron bed and either stretched or cut their legs to fit its length

prodromus or **prodrome** a forerunner; a precursor; a premonitory symptom; a preliminary course or publication

proem preface; introduction; prelude

profluent flowing forward; abundant; flowing smoothly

profulgent shining forth; brilliant; effulgent

prolation the act of prolating or pronouncing; utterance; pronunciation **prolix** wordy

prolusion a prelude; an introductory essay or exercise

promethean of or pertaining to Prometheus; life-giving; inspiring; boldly creative

Prometheus Titan chained to Mount Caucasus by Zeus for giving fire (stolen from heaven) to mankind

pronk to leap straight up with arched back, as the South African antelope; to prance or strut

proplasm a preliminary model or mold; a matrix

propylaeum or **propylon** a vestibule or portico, esp. to a temple

prosimetrum (pl. **prosimetra**) poetic composition that utilizes both prose and verse

protomartyr the first martyr for a particular cause

protomorphic having the most primitive character; in the earliest form   **protuberant** swelling; bulging out

provenience origin; source; place where found or produced; provenance; esp. used in the fine arts and archeology

proxemics study of the need for and the effects of physical distance (personal space) between people in different cultures and societies

Prufrockian weary, timid, indecisive and regretful

psammous sandy or gritty

psellism indistinct pronunciation; a stammer or lisp

pseudaesthesia false or imaginary feeling or sense perception, esp. as imagined in an amputated limb

pseudoblepsis false sight; imaginary vision of objects; hallucination

pseudopod(ium) any protoplasmic filament or irregular process projecting from a unicellular organism, or from any animal or plant cell, usually serving as an organ of locomotion or prehension

psilosopher a superficial or narrow pretender to philosophy; a sham philosopher

psithurism the sound of wind in trees or of rustling leaves; whispering sound

psychagogic attractive; encouraging; leading the soul; convincing someone to agree or follow

psychagogue a necromancer; one who communicates with the dead for some purpose

psychogenesis the origin and development of psychological processes such as personality and behavior, or more broadly, of the mind or soul

psychogenic originating in the mind or in mental or emotional conflict, rather than being of physiological origin

psychomachy a conflict between soul and body

psychomancy necromancy; divination by conversing with the souls of the dead

psychopannychism the doctrine that the soul falls asleep at death and does not wake until the body's resurrection

psychotaxis involuntary change of mental outlook to satisfy the personality

psychrophilic capable of living in relatively low temperatures

psychrophobia an abnormal sensitivity to, or fear of, the cold; esp. cold water

pterosaur any species of the extinct order of flying reptiles Pterosauria, such as the pterodactyl

pubarche beginning of puberty, esp. as defined by the first appearance of pubic hair

pudendum the external genital organ of a human; esp. the female's vulva   **pudibund** shameful; prudish

pudor an appropriate sense of modesty or shame; "Woman, undoing with sweet pudor her belt of rushrope, offers her allmoist yoni to man's lingam" – Joyce

puerperal pertaining to childbirth   **pukka** or **pucka** genuine

pule a plaintive, melancholy whine; to whine or whimper

pullulate to swarm; to teem; to multiply abundantly; to sprout

pulverulent consisting of, or reducible to, fine powder; covered with dust; powdery

purblind nearly blind; obtuse

purfle to decorate with a flowered border; to embroider; a decorative border or trim

purlicue the flourish at the end of a pen stroke; the end of a discourse; the distance between forefinger and thumb when extended

purlieu a place one frequents; an outlying or adjacent area; environs; neighborhood

purple passages or **purple patch** a particularly rich, ornate or fanciful part of a written work

purple prose a too ornate or highflown piece of writing

purpureal purple **purpurescent** tinged with purple

pursy fat and short-breathed; fat, short, and thick; swelled with pampering; characterized by a haughtiness born of being rich **puissant** powerful; strong; mighty

putid rotten; fetid; stinking; base; worthless

putrilage products or remnants of putrefaction or decay

putsch a coup; a secretly plotted, sudden attempt to overthrow the government of a nation

pycnomorphous or **pycnomorphic** compact; densely packed

pygephanous flashing one's buttocks; mooning

pygophilous an admirer of the human fundament

pyrexical feverish or relating to fever

pyrogen a substance that induces fever

pyrognomic easily made incandescent, esp. said of certain minerals **pyromancy** divination by means of fire

pythogenic produced by, or originating from, filth

pythonic relating to divination; prophetic; like an oracle; python-like, huge, monstrous [Greek python (spirit of divination)] **qasida** an elegiac or satirical Arabic poem

quab to shake; to quiver; a quagmire; an unfledged bird

quackle to suffocate; to choke

quadrennium a period of four years

quadrivial having four roads that meet at one place

quakebuttock a quisling; a coward

qualtagh first person you meet after leaving home, esp. on New Year's Day

quagswag to shake back and forth

quaquaversal in geology, dipping in all directions toward a center; facing every direction at once

quarterlight a small, pivoted, triangular window in a car used for ventilation **quasihemisemidemiquaver** a 128th note

quassation act of shaking or being shaken

quatch squat; flat

quaternity the number four; a group of four, esp. concept of God consisting of four persons

quatervois crossroads

quebrada a ravine or gorge, esp. in Latin America

quercine of or pertaining to oak trees

querencia an area in the bull-ring where the bull feels strong and safe **querent** or **querist** questioner; inquirer

querimonious prone to complaining

querken to stifle or choke

quersprung in skiing, a jumpturn in which the skis land at right angles to the poles **quesited** inquired about

quickhatch or **queequehatch** wolverine or carcajou

quiddity an eccentricity; the essence, nature, or particular distinction of a thing; a quibble

quiddler one who wastes time; an idler or dawdler at work; esp. when such idling interferes with other people working

quidnunc one who is curious about what's going on in the social scene; a nosy person

quilling a linen or other fabric border folded to resemble a row of quills

quincunx arrangement of 5 objects with 4 at the corners of a square and the 5th at the center

quisby someone who does not work

quisquilious composed of rubbish or rubbish-like; valueless

quixotry visionary schemes; quixotic behavior

quonking or **quonk** an accidental noise that disturbs or disrupts a television or radio program due to proximity to the microphones or cameras

quotha indeed; forsooth [an interjection] **quotidian** daily

Rabelaisian like Rabelais or his writings; marked by grotesque humor or extravagant caricature

rackrent demand of the highest possible rent; high rent

raffish resembling a raff, or a man of low character; worthless; disreputable, rakish

ragmatical wild; riotous   **rakehell** a lewd, dissolute fellow; a debauchee; a rake; immoral

rakish dissolute; lewd; debauched; possessing a careless look; dashing

rallentando in music, a slackening; a gradual decrease in tempo; ritardando

ramage boughs or branches of a tree; wild; untamed

rampallian a scoundrel; a wretch

rampasture a communal dorm room for unmarried men

rampick or **rampike** a standing dead tree, esp. a skeletal tree or a splintered trunk killed by wind, lightning, or fire

rapine the seizure of someone's property by force; plunder; ravishment   **raptus** rapture; ecstasy

rara avis a rare, unique or extraordinary person or thing

rasorial scratching the ground for food

rastaquouere a social climber who tries too hard to be in fashion

rataplan the iterative sound of beating a drum, or of a galloping horse; any drumming sound

ratbaggery nonsense; unconventional behavior; weirdness

rathskeller a bar or restaurant below street level, esp. one that serves beer

ravening eager for plunder; rapacious; greedily devouring

ravin ravenous

razzmatazz ambiguous or meaningless language; empty and tiresome speculation; something presenting itself in a fanciful & showy way, esp. when intended to impress & confuse   **rebarbative** repellent; irritating

recherché sought out with care; choice; of rare quality, elegance, or attractiveness; unique and refined

reckling a weak child or animal, esp. the weakest of the brood, or litter

recumbentibus a knockdown blow, either verbal or physical

recusant one who is obstinate in refusal, esp. to authority;

one standing out stubbornly against general practice or opinion

redivivus living again; brought back to life; revived

refection refreshment after hunger or fatigue; a repast; a lunch; a light meal

refluent flowing back; returning; ebbing

refulgent casting a bright light; radiant; brilliant; resplendent; shining; splendid

reginal queen-like or relating to a queen

regnant exercising regal authority; reigning, as a queen regnant; having the chief power; ruling; predominant

regolith the layer of loose rocky material lying above bedrock

reify to regard an abstract thing as a real concrete thing

reiver or **reaver** one who takes away by violence or by stealth; robber; pillager; plunderer

reliction a recession of the sea or other water, leaving dry land; land left uncovered by such recession

reliquary a depository, often a small box or casket, in which relics are kept

relucent reflecting light; shining; glittering; glistening; bright; luminous; splendid

remembrancer someone or something that reminds one of something

remontado someone who has left civilization and gone to the hills, mountains or deep forest [literally re-mounted]

remontant rising again – applied to roses that bloom more than once a season

remplissage something that just fills up space, esp. filling used in music and literature   **remuda** herd of horses

renitent resisting pressure; acting against impulse by elastic force; persistently opposed

repine to feel inward discontent; to complain discontentedly

replevin in law, a personal action to recover possession of goods wrongfully taken

reproof blame expressed to the face; censure for a fault; rebuking **reprove**

reptant in biology, creeping or crawling

residuum same as residue

respire to breathe; to take rest from toil; to rest

reticular having the form of a net or network; formed with interstices; retiform; intricate

retrocognition extrasensory knowledge of past events

retrophilia an abiding love for things of the past

retrosexual the opposite of the metrosexual, a man who adopts a traditional masculine style in dress and manners and spends little time or money altering his appearance

revalescent growing well; recovering strength; convalescent

revanche revenge; a nation's or ethnic group's political policy of regaining lost territory **revanchist**

revenant someone who returns from a long absence; a person or thing reborn; a supernatural being that comes back to life; a zombie or ghost

reviviscent reviving; regaining or restoring life or action

rhapsodomancy divination by means of verses, esp. by randomly opening poetry books

rhinocerial very heavy; pertaining to, or resembling, the rhinoceros

rhinocerotic of or pertaining to the rhinoceros

rident laughing **ridley** can refer to two species of sea turtle

rima a narrow and elongated aperture; a cleft; a fissure

rimose full of rimes, fissures, or chinks

rimple to rumple; to wrinkle

rindle a small water course or gutter

rivage shore or coast; "From the green rivage many a fall / Of diamond rillets musical" –Tennyson

rivel to contract into wrinkles; to shrivel; to shrink; a wrinkle

riven split, torn asunder **roche** rock or cliff; a rocky height

roister to bluster; to swagger; to bully; to be bold, noisy, vaunting, or turbulent

romantic suggesting emotion aroused by that which appeals to the imagination as it is influenced by the idealization of life in literature, art, etc. **rorid** dewy

roriferous producing dew   **rorifluent** flowing with dew
rorulent full of, or abounding in, dew
roscid containing, or consisting of, dew; dewy
rosmarine a fabulous walrus-like sea animal which was
    reported to climb by means of its teeth to the tops of rocks
    to feed upon the dew   **roughcast** plaster
rubescent growing or becoming red; tending to redness
rudesby an uncivil, turbulent fellow
rufescent tinged red or reddish
rumen the first of a ruminant creature's stomachs
rumpy-pumpy sexual activity
rupestrine or **rupicolous** in zoology and botany, growing or
    existing on or among rocks; saxicoline
rupestral composed of, or engraved in, rock
rusticate to dwell or reside in the country; to compel to
    reside in the country
rusticity rustic manners; rudeness; coarseness; simplicity;
    artlessness
ruth sorrow for another's misery; pity; tenderness **ruthful**
rutilant having a reddish glow; shining
sabkha an area of coastal salt flats, esp. in North Africa and
    Arabia
sabrage the opening of a bottle by slicing off the bottle's
    neck with a saber sword
sabulous sandy; gritty; growing a sandy area
saeter or **shieling** a mountain meadow or pasture used
    seasonally for grazing milk cows or goats
sagittal of or pertaining to an arrow; resembling an arrow;
    furnished with an arrow-like appendage
salariat salary earners as a group or a class
salina a salt marsh or pond
salmagundi a miscellaneous assortment; a mixture
salmanazar a wine bottle holding the volume equivalent to
    about 12 normal bottles
saltant leaping; jumping; dancing **saltation**
samsara in Hinduism and Buddhism, the ongoing cycle of

birth, death, and rebirth endured by human beings and all other mortal beings, and from which release is obtained by achieving the highest enlightenment

sanatory conducive to health; tending to cure; healing; curative; sanative

sang froid or **sangfroid** or **sang-froid** composure, level-headedness, coolness in trying circumstances

sanguicolous living in blood

sanguinolent containing or tinged with blood

sanguisugent blood-sucking

sanguivorous subsisting upon blood

sapid or **sipid** possessing flavor; tasty; savory

sapiential having or imparting wisdom

saporific able to produce the sensation of taste; producing taste, flavor, or relish   **sapphic** lesbian

saprogenic causing or resulting from putrefaction

saprophilous or **saprophytic** feeding or growing upon decaying animal or vegetable matter

saprostomous having bad breath

sapwood the alburnum, or soft tissue beneath tree bark

saraband a slow Spanish dance of Saracenic origin; the triple time music so danced to

sarcenet a type of fine silk fabric

sarcoid resembling flesh or muscle   **sarcoline** flesh-colored

sarcophile a carnivorous animal

sarcophilous or **sarcophagous** prone to eating flesh

sardanapalian luxuriously effeminate, like Sardanapalus in a play by Byron of the same name

sardonic derisive, mocking, malignant, or bitterly sarcastic [after Sardinia, a large island in the Mediterranean – eating a Sardinian plant was believed to produce facial convulsions as if in a maniacal laughter]

sarky sarcastic [British]

sastrugi ridges of irregular design in snow running parallel to prevailing wind direction

saturnalia a period or occasion of general license, in which the passions or vices have riotous indulgence; a particularly riotous, and esp. drink or drug heavy, party [from the ancient Roman festival of Saturn during which class distinctions including slavery were temporarily suspended]

saturnine heavy; grave; gloomy; dull

satyagraha the policy of nonviolent resistance to political oppression developed by Gandhi

satyaloka in Hindu mythology, the highest heaven [Sanskrit (world of truth)]

satyrid species of butterfly

satyromania extreme sexual desire and behavior in men

sault falls or rapids in a river

sawm in Islam, the abstention of food and drink during daylight hours of the month of Ramadan

saxatile of or pertaining to rocks; living among rocks

saxicavous boring, or hollowing out, rocks

saxicolous growing on or among rocks

saxifragous dissolving or breaking stone

scagliola imitation marble

scambling in a haphazard or hasty manner, esp. eating a meal in such a manner

scandent of plants, having a tendency to climb whilst growing

scansorial climbing; adapted especially for climbing

scantling a small amount; the dimensions of a piece of lumber or building material

scapegrace a rogue; a man or boy of reckless and unprincipled habits; an incorrigible scamp

scaphism an old Persian method of executing criminals by installing them in a hollow tree and then covering them with honey to attract wasps and other insects

scazon limping verse   **scherm** a type of hut in South Africa

schlockmeister a merchant of inferior products; seller of cheap goods   **Schmiergeld** a bribe [German]

schnozzle or **schnozzola** a human nose, esp. a large one

schussboomer a fast and skilled downhill skier

schwerpunkt the focal point; a point of maximum effort, esp. in a military operation [German schwer (weighty) + Punkt (point)]

scintilla a spark; the least particle; an iota

scintillant producing sparks

scintillation the act of scintillating; emitting sparks; sparkling; twinkling; a radiant display of wit

scintillescent sparkling or twinkling

sclaff in golf, to hit the ground before the ball, resulting in a very bad shot

sclerotic hard; firm; indurated; in anatomy, applied to the firm outer coat of the eyeball

scopic visual   **scrag** something thin, lean, or rough; a bony piece, esp. a bony neckpiece of meat

scranch to grind with the teeth, with a crackling sound; to craunch (crush with the teeth)

scribacious fond of writing; prone to excessive writing

scribomania or **graphomania** a strong urge to write

scrimer one skilled at fencing or swordplay

scrimshank to shirk duty

scrippage the contents of a scrip, or wallet; baggage

scriptorium in an abbey or monastery, the room set apart for writing or copying manuscripts; a room devoted to writing

scriptory of or pertaining to writing; expressed in writing, rather than verbally

scripturient having a fervent desire for writing

scrofulous morally degenerate; corrupt

scrotiform purse-shaped; pouch-shaped

scrooch or **scrootch** to crouch or huddle, often followed by down, up or in

scry to predict the future using crystal balls; descry

sea smoke fog over the ocean, caused by cold air moving over warmer water   **secern** to separate; to distinguish

secreta products of secretion, as by an organ

selcouth rarely known; unusual; strange; marvelous

selenophobia fear of the moon

selkie a creature that is seal-like in water, but human on land

selva a rain forest in a tropical area, esp. the Amazon basin

semilunate or **semilunar** shaped like a half-moon

seminiferous seed-bearing; producing seed

semispheric having the form of half a sphere

semitaur mythical creature that is half-man, half-bull

sempervirent evergreen; always fresh

sempiternal everlasting; endless; having beginning, but no
end; eternal; "When lost within the gloam of that summer's
sempiternal seeming..."

senectitude old age

senescent growing old; decaying with the lapse of time

sennight the space of seven nights and days, a week

sensibilia things that can be perceived by the senses

separatrix something that separates; virgule or separating
slash mark

septemfluous flowing sevenfold; divided into seven streams
or currents

septenary lasting or continuing seven years; consisting of, or
relating to, seven

septentrional northern; pertaining to the north

sepulchral of or pertaining to burial or the grave; funereal;
gloomy

sequacious inclined to follow; pliant; attendant; servile
[Latin sequax (inclined to follow), from sequi (to follow)]

sequela a secondary consequence; a follower, as of a sect;
that which follows from reason

serac a sharp ridge of ice on a glacier

seraglio a harem; a place for keeping wives or concubines;
a place of licentious pleasure

seraph (pl. **seraphim**) one of an order of celestial beings, each
having three pairs of wings;
"As full, as perfect, in vile man that mourns,
As the rapt seraph that adores and burns." – Pope

seraphic of or relating to a seraph; pure; sublime; blissful;
angelic

serein usually in the tropics, a mist or very light rain that falls from a clear sky soon after sunset   **seric** silken

seriocomic having both serious and comedic qualities or tendencies

serotine occurring later than average or normal, esp. late flowering; a species of bat

serotinal late to develop, esp. of late flowering plants; relating to or occurring in late summer

serpentry a winding motion like a serpent's; a place inhabited or infested by serpents; a type of behavior attributed to snakes; any act or motion of a serpent or serpent like creature; collective term for all serpents

sesquipedalian a very long word or person who uses same

shambolic chaotic, disorganized or mismanaged

shamus a private detective

Shangri-la a place of complete bliss, delight, and peace, esp. such a place that is also remote and isolated; paradise [after Shangri (a coined place name in the novel Lost Horizon) + Tibetan la (a mountain pass)]

Shaxpeer or **Shexpere** alternate spellings for Shakespeare's name that he used himself

shebang any matter of present concern, thing, or business

sheep's eyes a secretive, pining or amorous look; a humble, doting glance

shemozzle a state of chaos or confusion; a muddle; a quarrel or rumpus

shibboleth a shibboleth is a watchword or sound used to distinguish outsiders from those that belong to a particular class or group

shot-clog a bore who is tolerated because he buys drinks

shrike a predatory songbird; shriek

shrimping spooning, but in a pronounced fetal position

shrive to hear the confession of someone and give absolution

sidereal relating to the stars; starry; astral

siffilate to speak in a whisper

sightworthy meriting looking at

sigil a seal, signature, or signet; a sign, image or symbol considered to be magical

silva or **sylva** the forest trees of a region or country, considered collectively; a description or history of the forest trees of a country [Latin, silva (forest)]

silvan or **sylvan** pertaining to the forest or woodlands; residing in a forest; covered in forest

silvicolous growing in woodlands

silviculture growing of trees; forestry

simoon a strong, hot, sandy wind in Arabia or Northern Africa

sine qua non an essential or indispensable element, condition, or ingredient [Latin (without which not)]

sinistral of, on, or facing the left side; left-handed

sinistrodextral from left to right

sinter to compact and heat a powder to form a solid mass

sirenic or **sirenical** alluring and/or tempting; melodious

sirocco an oppressive, hot wind, esp. one from the Libyan deserts felt in southern Europe

sisyphean incessant or incessantly recurring, but futile

sith since; in later times

sitzfleisch the ability to endure or carry on with an activity

sitzkreig a non-shooting war; wartime without violence; a cold war

sitzpinkler literally, a man who pees sitting down; an unmanly man; man dominated by wife or girlfriend [German]

skald Scandinavian bard

skelder to deceive; to cheat; to trick

skelic of, like or pertaining to the skeleton

skepsis doubt or disbelief; skepticism

skerrick a very small amount or portion, often with negative connotation **skerry** rocky small island

Skidbladnir in Norse Mythology, a ship drafted by two dwarfs that was large enough to hold all the gods, always had a favorable wind, and could be collapsed to pocket size

skirl to produce a shrill sound, such as bagpipes

skookum excellent; impressive; strong; durable

skosh a tiny amount; a little bit; tad; smidgen; jot [Japanese sukoshi (a little)]   **skyline** horizon

slade a little dell or valley; a flat piece of low, moist ground

slaver to smear with saliva issuing from the mouth; to defile with drivel; to slabber; to be besmeared with saliva; to fawn

sleech slimy mud or sludge; a coastal mudflat

slickenside in geology, a rock surface polished smooth by friction or produced from cleavage

slivercasting a video broadcast targeting a very narrow audience

sloke edible algae; a type of seaweed; slime or scum in water

slubberdegullion a low-minded, dirty wretch

slugabed one who indulges in lying abed; a sluggard

slumberous inviting slumber; soporiferous; being in the repose of slumber; sleepy; drowsy; "Pensive in the slumberous shade." – Pope

slummock to lumber; to walk with heavy and awkward movements; a slovenly individual

slurvian speech, esp. English speech, that is notably slurred or sloppily pronounced

smaragdine pertaining to or resembling emeralds; emerald color

smegmatic being of the nature of soap; soapy; cleansing; detersive

snaffle to take for oneself, esp. In a devious manner

snarf to eat greedily; to expel food or drink through the nose accidentally, as when failing to suppress laughter; to fall asleep without taking off one's clothes

snarky rude sarcasm, usually arising from irritation and often humorously delivered

snickersnee a knife that looks like a small sword

sniggle fish for eels; to catch an eel with a baited hook

snobocracy government of snobs

snollygoster a dishonest or sleazy politician or lawyer

snowblink a glare on the earthward side of clouds that is reflected from snow on the surface

snowbroth snow and water mixed; very cold liquor

snuffle breathing noisily through a partially blocked nose

snuggery a snug, cozy place

snurt sneezing with an attendant expulsion of mucus

solfatara a volcanic vent that emits sulfurous vapors

solferino purplish-red

soliloquacious wont to give soliloquies

soliterraneous pertaining to both the sun and the earth, esp. their collective effects   **solivagant** wandering alone

solus alone   **somatism** materialism

somewhither to some indeterminate place; to some place or other   **somnial** of, like or relating to dreams

somniate to dream; to make sleepy

somniferous causing or inducing sleep; soporific; dormitive; as, a somniferous potion   **somnific** causing sleep

somniloquy talking while asleep; words spoken during sleep

somnolent sleepy; drowsy; inclined to sleep; causing sleep

somnolescent half-asleep

Somnus Roman god of sleep [Night his father, Death his twin]

soothfast firmly fixed in the truth; true; genuine; real; faithful

sophistry fallacious reasoning; reasoning sound in appearance only

soporose or **soporous** causing sleep; sleepy; in a very deep sleep [Latin sopor (a deep sleep)]

sortilege the act or practice of drawing lots; divination by drawing lots; also, sorcery or witchcraft in general; enchantment

sough to make a soft rustling or murmuring sound; such a sound; a sigh   **sovenance** remembrance; memory

spadassin swordsman [French spada (sword)]

spado a castrated animal; an impotent person

spagyric alchemical; a chemist

spall to break into small pieces; to splinter; a chip or splinter of stone, rock or ore

spatchcock to insert forcibly into a text too hastily or inappropriately; a fowl stuffed and cooked very soon after killing; to prepare something in haste, as for an emergency

spathe botany, the sheath around a blossom

spatiate to rove; to ramble

spectrophobia a morbid fear of mirrors and one's own reflection

specular having the qualities of a mirror; having a smooth, reflecting surface   **spelaean** cave-like; inhabiting caves

spelter zinc   **sphallolalia** flirtatious talk that leads nowhere

spherule a little sphere or spherical body

sphinx in mythology, a creature with the head of a person and the body of an animal, esp. a lion; someone who keeps their thoughts or intentions secret

sphingal of or like a sphinx

spicula (pl. **spiculum**) a little spike; a pointed and fleshy appendage

spiflicate to destroy; to beat severely; to confound; to stifle

spiloma a mole; a birthmark; a naevus

spilth a spillage; spilled material

spindrift sea spray blown from the tops of waves; snow blowing off a mountain peak

spiracle a pore or opening, used esp. by spiders and some fish for breathing; the blowhole of a whale; any small aperture or vent for air or other fluid

spirant in phonetics, a fricative; any sound produced by air flowing through a constriction in the oral cavity and typically producing a sibilant, hissing or buzzing quality, as an S or F sound in English

spiration the act of breathing

spirituelle possessing an ethereal nature; refined; pure

spirulate in zoology, having spirally arranged color spots or structural parts

spizzerinctum nerve, guts, zeal, determination, ardor

splanchnic visceral; intestinal

splenetic ill-humored; malicious; spiteful; fretful

splodge a spot or stain of irregular shape; splotch

spoliate to plunder; to pillage; to despoil; to rob

spoondrift or **spindrift** water sprayed into the air by wind at sea   **spoonmeat** soft food

sprachgefuhl the instinctive or intuitive grasp of the natural idiom of a language

sprezzatura performing a difficult task with grace and ease; effortlessness; nonchalance

springal or **springald** a youth; a stripling

spruit a stream or river branch

spume foam, froth or scum on water, esp. on sea water

spumescence frothiness; the state of foaming

spumescent resembling froth or foam; foaming

spumid spumous; frothy   **sputum** that which is spat

squab fat; thick; bulky; unfledged; unfeathered, as a squab pigeon   **squamous** scaly

squattocracy government by landowners, esp. those considered as squatters; in Australia, wealthy landowners considered as a class   **squib** a lampoon; to lampoon

squillion a large, indeterminate number, often used hyperbolically

starveling a person or thing severely lacking for food; hungry, lean, or pining with want of food

stat immediately, esp. in medical situations [abbreviation of the Latin term statim "immediately"]

stellate resembling a star

stelliferous having, or abounding with, stars

stellify to turn into a star; to cause to appear like a star; to place among the stars, or in heaven

steerage area of a ship having the poorest accommodations and occupied by passengers paying the lowest fare, usually aft and often in older ships near the rudder

Sterculius the God of manure and fertilizer

stillicide water falling in drops, esp. from the roof of a house or from icicles or stalactites

stochastic random; randomly determined; pertaining or akin to a series of random events

stodge heavy, bland food, esp. starch-based foods

stonk to bombard, esp. with artillery; a heavy dose of such bombardment

stonking awesome or amazing; powerful [British slang]

Storting the supreme legislature of Norway

stravage or **stravaige** stroll; meander; roam; wander

stridulate to make a shrill or musical sound, such as the males of many insects **stridulous**

strikhedonia the pleasure derived from being able to just say "to hell with it"

strobic appearing to spin; spinning

strumpetocracy government of prostitutes

sturmfrei having the house to oneself, as when parents or flatmates are away [German sturm (storm) + frei (free)]

stygian of or relating to the Styx, one of the four rivers of hell; infernal; dark and gloomy **suasion** the act of persuading

suaviloquent sweetly speaking; using agreeable speech

subaerial located or occurring at the Earth's surface, esp. on land **subastral** beneath the stars; terrestrial

subboreal very cold

subcelestial beneath the heavens; terrestrial

subception subconscious senses

subderisorious ridiculing in a loving manner; ridiculing with moderation or delicacy

subdolous sly; crafty; cunning; artful; secretly deceitful

subduct to withdraw; to take away

subfocal describing a thing one is not entirely conscious of

subfuscous or **subfusk** or **subfusc** dusky; darkish; drab

subitize to perceive the number of objects in a group rapidly without counting them individually

subito in haste; quickly; rapidly; immediately

subjacent lying under or below; being situated lower, as hills and subjacent valleys

subjoin append; to add at the end of something

sublunary pertaining to this world; earthly; terrestrial

submerse submerge

submontane located at or near the base of a mountain; of or like foothills; passing thru or under mountains

subnascent growing underneath **subniveal** under snow

subnubilar under clouds

subtend to extend under so as to enclose or surround

subternatural less than natural

subtopia suburban areas around cities lacking individuality

subtrist somewhat sad

subventaneous produced by the wind

succuba or **succubus** a female demon that connects sexually
with sleeping men [pl. **succubi**]

sudatorium or **sudatory** a hot room used to induce sweating

sudoral sweaty; of or relating to sweat

sudorific that causes perspiration

sudoriparous or **sudoriferous** sweaty; secreting perspiration

sufflate to blow up; to inflate; to inspire

sugent sucking; suctorial; designed or evolved for sucking

suggilated beaten until bruised **sumpter** a pack animal

sundowner hobo; itinerant worker

supercrescent growing on something else that is also
growing

superfuse to pour (something) over or on something else

superincumbent lying or resting on top of something else;
overlying; overhanging

superjacent positioned immediately above or on top of
something else; overlying

superlunary otherworldly; situated beyond or above the
moon; translunary

supernatant floating on the surface of a liquid

supersensible or **supersensual** spiritual; beyond the reach of
the human senses **superstruct** to build on top of

supervene to follow right after something; to ensue; to
supercede; to be dependent upon an earlier occurrence; to
be dependent on something for existence or truth

supine lying on one's back; sloping, as of land

supraciliary of or pertaining to the eyebrows

supraliminal conscious

supralunar beyond the moon; figuratively, very lofty

supramundane above or beyond our world; celestial [Latin supra-(above) + mundus (world)]

supranatural supernatural   **surd** deaf; unheard; voiceless

surquedry or **surquidry** overweening pride; arrogance

suspiration the act of breathing, not necessarily for a sustained period; sighing

sussultatory characterized by vertical oscillations of large amplitude – often referencing earthquakes

susurrant (said of voices or sounds) gently whispering; murmured; soft

susurrous whispering, rustling, full of whispering, hissing or murmuring sounds

susurrus a whispering or rustling sound; a murmur; "The soft susurrus and sighs of the branches" – Longfellow

sutra a rule or formula, esp. in Sanskrit grammar or Hindu law or philosophy; an aphorism, esp. a Buddhist one [Sanskrit sutra (thread)]

Svengali one who manipulates or controls another as by some mesmeric or sinister influence, esp. a coach, mentor or industry mogul [after Svengali, a musician and hypnotist, in the novel Trilby written by George du Maurier]

swallet a sinkhole

swanskin the skin of a swan with the down or feathers on; a type of brushed flannel cotton twill fabric

swarth a sward; a wraith

swash the water that washes ashore after a wave has broken; in typography, a long protruding ornamental line or pen stroke; a bar over-washed by the sea; a ripple on a liquid's surface

sweven a vision; a dream [Old English swefn (sleep, dream, vision)]

swingletree or **whippletree** a wooden crossbar for a plow or carriage pulled by horse or ox

swink to labor; to toil; to slave

swith promptly; quickly; strongly; vehemently

swive to copulate with a woman

sybarite one who indulges in or is dedicated to pleasures or luxuries **sybaritic**

sybilline or **sibylline** of or pertaining to a sibyl or female oracle; having oracle-like powers of prediction; clairvoyant; mysterious

syllogism in logic, an inference in which one proposition (the conclusion) follows necessarily from two other propositions, known as the premises **syllogistic**

sylph in mythology, an elemental being of air, usually female; a slender woman or girl, esp. a graceful and sublime one

sylvatic of or pertaining to woods or woodland organisms; sylvan; of or pertaining to wild animals

sylvestral of, pertaining to, similar to, or growing in trees or forests

sympatric in biology, species or populations living in the same geographic area, but not interbreeding

symphoric clumsy or accident prone

symphysis the fusion of once separate parts, esp. in anatomy; bones growing together

symposiarch master of a feast; toastmaster; master of a symposium

synanthy in botany, the abnormal fusion of two or more flowers

syncretism a combination of two systems of thought or belief

syndetic in grammar, connected by a conjunction or serving to connect; connective in general

syrinx a set of pan-pipes; a narrow channel cut in rock, esp. in ancient Egyptian tombs **syrt** a quicksand or bog

syrtic boggy; resembling quicksand

syzygy in astronomy, the alignment of three or more celestial bodies; in psychology, an archetypal pairing of contrasexual opposites (one arising from the anima, one from the animus), symbolizing the communication of the conscious and unconscious minds; any pair of closely related things

tabescent wasting away; becoming emaciated; shriveling

tactual of or relating to the sense of touch; tactile

talus an ankle bone; in geology, a sloping heap of fragments of rock lying at the foot of a precipice

tanglery the upper regions of a dense forest, esp. a rain forest, where the branches and leaves of trees and other foliage intertwine

tantalism a punishment like that of Tantulus; a teasing or tormenting by the hope or near approach of good which is not attainable; tantalization

tantara a flourish on a trumpet

tantivy swiftly; speedily; rapidly; at full gallop

taratantara the onomatopoeia of a particular sound made by a bugle or trumpet

tarantism an extreme urge to dance, popularly thought to have been caused by the bite of a tarantula and prevalent in southern Italy in the 15th through 17th centuries

tarboosh a red cap sometimes worn by Turks and others, either alone or swathed with linen to make a turban

tarradiddle a trivial lie; silly talking or writing

tartuffe a religious hypocrite

technomania great enthusiasm for modern technology

tegular looking like tiles; laid out like tiles

telary of or relating to a web; spinning webs; retiary

telegnosis knowledge of events outside of normal sensory perception; clairvoyance

telesthesia the perception of events that are beyond normal sensory limits

tellurian of, relating to, or inhabiting the Earth; terrestrial

telluric terrestrial; pertaining to the Earth

telos aim; ultimate purpose; end of a goal-driven process

temenos a piece of land cut off and assigned as an official domain, esp. to kings and chiefs; a piece of land separated from common uses and dedicated to a god, a sanctuary or holy grove

temperative having the power to serve as a tempering, or moderating, influence   **temulency** drunkenness

tenebrific gloomy; obscure   **tenebrous** dark and gloomy

tenebrose dark; tenebrous; obscure or obtuse; morally, culturally or mentally benighted

tephra the solid material thrown into the air by volcanic eruption that settles on the surrounding areas

teraph an image of a Semitic household god

termagant a quarrelsome, scolding woman, esp. one who is also old and shrewish

terraqueous of a celestial body, comprising both land and water, like the Earth

terremotive relating to an earthquake or movement of the earth

terriculament a source or object of needless or uncontrollable fear; a bugbear

terrigenous Earthborn; produced by the earth; in geology, derived from erosion of land-based rocks

tessellated covered with pieces that are similarly shaped

tetchy peevish; testy; easily annoyed or irritable

tetralemma a perplexity with four possible alternatives

tetramerous consisting of four parts, esp. in botany

tetrapolis four cities, grouped or allied together

thalassian marine; related to the sea or ocean; any sea tortoise   **thalassic** of or relating to seas and oceans

thalassocracy maritime supremacy

thalassophobia fear of the sea   **thanatophobia** fear of dying

thanatopsis contemplation of death

thanatosis gangrene; necrosis; the act of feigning death; in zoology, the ability of an animal to play dead to escape predators   **thaumaturge** a magician

theanthropic both human and divine

thenar the fleshy part at the base of the thumb

theolepsy seizure or possession of a mortal by a god or deity

theomania the belief that one is either God or chosen by God for a certain mission

theopantism belief that God constitutes the only reality

theopathy the emotional experience arising from religious belief

theophany a visible incarnation of God or a god to a mortal **theophanic**

theophilanthropism love of both God and humankind

theopneustic divinely inspired

thewless cowardly; lacking energy

thigmotropism the reflex of a plant (or other organism) to move when touched

thrasonic or **thrasonical** boastful; bragging

threnodic mournful

threnody an ode or song of lament; dirge

throttlebottom a harmless incompetent that holds a public office

thrum to speak with monotonous intonation; to idly strum a stringed musical instrument

thumomancy divination through the agency of one's own soul

thundersnow a thunderstorm with snow instead of rain

thunderstone a thunderbolt; any of the various stones regarded in some myths as having been cast to the earth as thunderbolts, such as meteorites and some ancient artifacts **thurification** the burning of incense

thymogenic due to emotion

thymoleptic psychologically energizing

thyrsus (pl. **thyrsi**) a pinecone-tipped, ivy-entwined staff carried by Dionysus and his followers

tigrine of, like or pertaining to tigers

timbrous resonant; sonorous

tinctumutation the dynamic variation in color of certain animals such as chameleons or cephalopods

tin god a person that abuses his or her authority over others, esp. in petty ways; a very self-important or self-righteous person; someone that considers themselves infallible and attempts to mandate standards of thought or action

Titanism revolt or defiance against established social or artistic norms

Titanomachy in Greek mythology, the 10 year war between the Titans and the Olympians, fought long before mankind existed, to decide who would rule the Universe [lower case, any battle of the gods]

titivate to make small improvements or alterations to one's appearance, a room, etc.; spruce up

toadstone a small stone, once believed to have grown inside a toad's head, worn as an amulet

toft a small hill; a grove of trees **tommyrot** nonsense

tonant or **tonitruous** thundering

tongue-shot distance that voices can be heard; voice-range; ear-shot

tonsorial of or pertaining to a barber or shaving

toothsome delicious **toparch** ruler of a place or country

topaz dark yellow color, like that of the gemstone

tophaceous gritty; sandy; rough; stony

toplofty high and mighty; self-important; haughty

topomancy divination using landforms

topophilia love for a certain place

tornadic like or pertaining to a tornado; capable of producing a tornado

torporific causing torpor, sluggishness, or inactivity

torrefy to dry by a fire; to dry or roast with any heat source; to subject to scorching heat

torrentine torrential; characterized by torrents; flowing heavily or in large quantities

Torschlusspanik the sense that time is running out due to age, e.g. a woman getting to old for childbirth [German (gate-shut panic)]

tosspot a toper; one habitually given to strong drink

tourbillion a vortex; a whirlwind; an ornamental firework which turns in the air, so as to form a scroll of fire

tovarish or **tovarisch** or **tovarich** comrade [Russian]

tracery any delicate ornamental work of interlacing lines or threads

trainspotter a person with great interest in trains or who counts trains; someone very interested in even the trivial information relating to a particular subject

traject to throw or cast through; to transmit

tralatitious transferred; passed down

Tramontane or **tramontane** classical name for a northern wind; anything that comes from the other side of mountains, esp. from north of the Alps; anything foreign, strange, or barbarous [Italian tramontana (beyond the mountains)]

transcalent pervious to, or permitting the passage of, heat

transcension the act of transcending

transfluent (of water or other liquid) flowing through or across something

transhumance seasonal migration of livestock (with herders) between two regions

translucid or **translucent** allowing light to pass through, but diffusing it; clear; lucid

translunary being or lying beyond the moon; ethereal; spiritual

transmarine lying or being beyond the sea; originating from across the sea

transpicuous easily understood, construed, or seen through; transparent

transpontine of, pertaining to, or situated on the far side of a bridge; of, or pertaining to the sensational melodramas presented on the south side of the Thames in the 19th century or earlier

transport to ravish with pleasure or ecstasy, as music transports the soul

transude to pass through a pore or membrane; to ooze or exude

transvection the act of conveying or carrying over; act of supernatural flight, like on a flying carpet

transvolation the act of flying beyond or across; flying higher than usual

travertine a type of limestone sometimes used for building

treen wooden tableware

treeware paper printed reading material as opposed to computer software   **tremulant** tremulous, trembling

treppenwitz a devastating rejoinder conceived only after leaving the place of debate; l'esprit d'escalier; afterwit; stairwit [German]   **tressilate** to quiver   **tribade** lesbian

tribology the science and technology of friction, lubrication, and wear

triboluminescence the production of light by friction

triffid a plant growing or spilling beyond normal bounds and seeming to overrun anything near by; anything that behaves in like manner [after triffids, a poisonous, mobile plant species in the 1951 science-fiction novel,The Day of the Triffids]

trilemma a quandary having three possible choices; a situation where it is difficult to decide which of three courses to pursue

trill in music, playing or singing two similar notes in quick succession

trimacular or **trimaculated** marked with three spots, or maculae   **trin** triplets or any group of three

trinoctial lasting three nights

tripartite divided into three parts; consisting of three parts; made between three parties

triphibious or **triphibian** on land, water and in the air, esp. said of military operations   **triste** sad

tristesse sadness; misery   **tristful** sad; sorrowful; gloomy

troilism the practice of engaging in sexual activity that includes three simultaneous participants

tropism in biology, the turning, either towards or away, of an organism in response to a stimulus

trothplight betrothed; espoused; affianced; plighted; to betroth; the act of betrothing

truckle to yield or bend obsequiously to the will of another; to submit

tufthunter a hanger-on to noble persons, or persons of quality, esp. in English universities; a toady

tumid swelled, enlarged, or distended; swelling in sound or sense; pompous; puffy; inflated; bombastic; falsely sublime

tumular consisting in a heap; formed or being in a heap or hillock; tumulus-shaped

tumulous or **tumulose** full of small hills or mounds; hilly

twee overly quaint, dainty, cute or nice [British – from a child's pronunciation of sweet]

twink to twinkle; to sparkle; to blink   **twitterlight** twilight

twizzle a turning, twisting or spinning motion; to rotate, spin or twirl   **tyloma** a callus

tyrian a shade of purple [from a dye rendered from mollusks in ancient Tyre]

ubermensch superman; a person with great powers [German (over man)]

uberous fruitful; copious; abundant; plentiful

uberty fertile growth; abundance; plenty; fruitfulness

ubication the quality or state of being in a place; position or location; whereness; ubiety

ubiety the state of existing in a specific point in space

ubique everywhere   **ucalegon** a neighbor whose house is on fire or has burned down   **ug** fear; terror

ugsome ugly; offensive; frightening; loathsome; "The horror and ugsomeness of death" – Latimer
[Middle English uggen (to fear, or inspire fear)]

ullage the amount which a vessel, as a cask, of liquor lacks of being full; wantage; deficiency; the amount (esp. of wine) abandoned unconsumed in glasses

ulterior situated beyond, or on the farther side; beyond what is obvious or evident; being intentionally concealed so as to deceive; happening after; subsequent

Ultima Thule the end of the world; the last extremity

ultraism extremism, esp. in politics

ultramontane being beyond or from beyond a mountain range, esp. the Alps

umami (u-mah-mee) one of the five basic tastes, the savory taste of foods such as seaweed, cured fish, aged cheeses and meats (the classic four tastes are sweet, sour, bitter and salty) [Japanese umami (sumptuousness)]

umbles entrails, esp. those of a deer

umbrageous having shade; shady; irritable; easily upset

umbratic or **umbratical** of or relating to the shade or darkness; shadowy

umbriferous casting or making a shade; umbrageous

umbrose shady   **Umwelt** the perception of one's surrounding environment [plural umwelten]

unberufen an injunction to fate that nothing will go wrong, esp. following boasting [German]

underbreath a soft voice; a whisper; a particularly unsubstantiated rumor

undercroft a subterranean room of any kind, esp. one under a church or one used for any sacred purpose; a vault or secret walk underground

undine a female water-sprite or nymph; the elemental being of water

ungual pertaining to or resembling a creature's nail, claw, or hoof; unguinal; in humans, of or pertaining to toenails or fingernails

unreeve to withdraw or remove, as a rope from an opening

untreasure to bring forth or give up, as things previously treasured; to remove, steal or destroy treasure; "The quaintness with which he untreasured, as by rote, the stores of his memory." – J. Mitford

upcast cast up; thrown upward; matter thrown up; a mine's outflow ventilating shaft

uprist uprising; in Christian theology, the resurrection

uranophobia a fear of heaven or the sky

uranoscopy observation of the heavens or heavenly bodies; astronomy

urbia a collective word for cities, esp. cities with dense populations

urbiculture way of life common in cities or urban areas

urgrund basis, foundation, cause or factor; a primal cause or ultimate cosmic principle [German ur- (primal) + grund (ground)]

urman coniferous forest, esp. swampy and esp. in Siberia

urtext the original version of a literary or musical work

usward or **uswards** toward us

vacillant vacillating; wavering; fluctuating; irresolute

vacua variant plural of vacuums

vafrous crafty; cunning; sly   **vagient** crying like a child

vagility in biology, the degree to which an organism moves within an environment

vaginate having or resembling a sheathe, esp. in biology; to sheathe, invaginate

vagitus the crying of a newborn baby; the cry of any wee child [Latin vagire (to wail)]

Valkyrie in Norse mythology, any of the female attendants of Odin, figures said to guide fallen warriors from the battlefield to Valhalla [old Norse valkyrja (chooser of the slain)]   **vaniloquent** chatting idly or speaking vainly

vastity emptiness or desolation; vastness, vastitude

vatic prophetic; pertaining to a prophet; oracular

vaticinate to predict or foretell

vaticide the murder, or the murderer, of a prophet

vavasor or **vavasour** a feudal subvassal, someone holding their lands from a vassal of the crown rather than from the crown directly

veduta a highly detailed, usually large-scale painting of a vista, esp. a cityscape

velarium a large awning, as over an ancient Roman theater

velation the act of covering with a veil or otherwise making secret or mysterious; secrecy

veldt or **veld** the open pasture land or grassland of South Africa [Afrikaans]

velivolant flying with sails; passing under full sail

velleity the lowest degree of desire or volition, with no attendant effort toward action; a slight wish not followed by any effort to obtain [Latin velle (to wish)]

velocipede a light carriage propelled by the feet; a bicycle

velutinous having a layer of soft short hairs, like velvet

venatic of, pertaining to or involved in hunting; taking pleasure in the chase

veneficial poisonous or pertaining to poison; malignant; sorcerous **venenate** to poison

ventifact rocks that have been abraded, pitted, etched, grooved, or polished by wind-driven sand or ice crystals

ventripotent fat; gluttonous; having a large appetite; eating with greedy delight **ventose** windy; flatulent

ventral of, pertaining to, or situated near, the belly; abdominal

ventricumbent lying on one's front or belly; prone

venust beautiful, esp. in an elegant way

verecund bashful; shy; modest

verglas a usually very slippery and nearly invisible film of ice over dark surfaces, such as pavement or water; black ice [French verre (glass) + glace (ice)]

verisimilitude quality of appearing to be real or true

verjuice a very acidic juice made by pressing unripe grapes; a sour disposition

vernalagnia the heightening of sexual desire or romantic feelings in Springtime

vernissage a private viewing of an art exhibition before it opens publicly

versal universal; in calligraphy, the ornamental letter that begins a section

versant the slope of a mountain or mountain ridge; the overall slope of a region

versicle in poetry and songs (esp. hymns), one of a series of lines that are shorter than a standard line of verse

versicolor multicolored or changing in color

vertical sonority in music, this refers to considering the relationships between pitches that occur together (usually this means at the same time) – harmony is the study of vertical sonorities

vertiginous having an aspect of great depth, drawing the eye to look downwards; inducing a feeling of giddiness, vertigo or whirling; pertaining to vertigo; revolving; rotating

vespertide or **eventide** evening

vespertilian of or relating to bats

vespertine of, related to, or occurring in the evening

vespiary a nest or colony of wasps

vespine of, pertaining to, or characteristic of wasps

vesture robe, clothing; a covering like clothing

Vesuvian of or relating to Italian Mount Vesuvius, which erupted in the year 79 and buried Pompeii; prone to any type of sudden and explosive outbursts

vetanda things that are forbidden

viatical of or pertaining to a journey or to traveling; viatic

viaticum provisions for a long trip

vibrissa any of the tactile whiskers on the nose of an animal, such as a cat; any similar feather near the mouth of some birds [Latin vibrissae (nostril hairs)]

vicennial occurring every twenty years; lasting twenty years

victress or **victoress** or **victrix** a female victor or conqueror

vigesimal a twentieth part; occurring in intervals of 20; relating to the number 20

vigesimation or **vicesimation** the destruction of one-twentieth of something, esp. the killing of every twentieth person, esp. by lottery

vigintillion a very, very large number; ten to the 63rd power

vilipend belittle; despise; to express a disparaging opinion of; to slander

villatic of or pertaining to a farm or village; rural

villose or **villous** velvety; covered with fine or woolly hairs; shaggy with soft hairs

vimen a long, slender, flexible twig, shoot or branch

vinolent very fond of drinking wine, esp. to excess

vinous of or pertaining to wine; having the quality of wine

violaceous of a violet color   **violous** violent

viperous of or pertaining to vipers; treacherous; venomous

virago a woman of extraordinary stature, strength, and courage; a masculine woman; a female warrior

virescent becoming green or greenish

virga visible streaks of rain or snow that evaporate before reaching the ground [Latin virga (rod, streak)]

viridian chrome green   **viridity** greenness; freshness

viripotent a sexually fit and mature man; a man reproductively able, or generally marriageable

virtu a love of, knowledge of, or taste for objects of fine art; objects of art collectively

visceral of or pertaining to the viscera; splanchnic; instinctive; dealing with deep or primal emotions, or "gut" feelings

viscid semi-fluid; sticky; glutinous; viscous; tenacious

viscountess a female viscount or wife of a viscount (ranked below earl or count, above baron)

vitelline like or relating to egg yolk; the color of egg yolk

vitellus an egg yolk

vituperable deserving of severe censure

vituperate to overwhelm with wordy abuse; to censure severely **vituperative**

vivific enlivening; vivifying   **vivificate** enliven

vivisepulture burying someone or something alive

vizard or **vizzard** a mask worn to disguise or protect the face; a pretense

vocable able to be spoken; a word considered as sound only, without meaning

vocabularian one who pays much, esp. too much, attention to words; one with a large vocabulary

volable nimble-witted   **volacious** apt or fit to fly

volplane a steep, controlled dive, esp. by an aircraft with the engine off; the act of so diving

volte-face a sudden reversal in policy or attitude

vomitorium a place where vomiting occurs; an exit to an amphitheater

vomitus vomit; that which has been expelled as vomit

voortrekker a Boer (or Afrikaner) pioneer, who trekked from Cape Colony into the hinterland of South Africa to establish the Transvaal and Orange Free State during the 1830's **vorago** abyss, chasm, gulf

vorant devouring; swallowing greedily

vorpal sharp or deadly [from the Lewis Carroll poem Jabberwocky]

vortical of, or pertaining to a vortex; containing vortices; moving in a vortex

vortiginous whirling; moving rapidly round a center; vortical

votive dedicated or given in fulfillment of a vow or pledge; of, expressing or symbolizing a vow

vril a controllable form of energy, capable of revolutionizing life on earth [from the 1871 science fiction novel *The Coming Race*]

vulgus the common people; the public; a throng or crowd

vulnerose full of wounds; wounded

vulviform like a cleft with projecting edges; vulva-shaped

waftage conveyance on a buoyant medium, as air or water

wafture act of waving or wafting; a wave-like motion

waldgrave a German noble title; formerly, a head forest keeper in the German empire

Waldsterben the destruction of the forest caused by environmental pollution [German (dying of the forest)]

waldo a remote manipulation system in which a slave device mimics the motions of a master device manipulated directly by the operator [from Waldo F. Jones, the inventor of such gadgets in a 1940 Heinlein sci-fi story]

wamble to move irregularly to and fro; to stagger

wampus a weird or somehow objectionable person

wanchancy unlucky

wanhope want of hope; despair; also, faint or delusive hope

wanweird an unhappy fate

wapinshaw or **wapinschaw** a periodic exhibition of weapons by all persons in a certain area that bear arms in order to demonstrate readiness for combat [Scottish]

waqf a charitable endowment of land for Islamic religious purposes

warison wealth; reward; punishment; a musical note, esp. on a bugle, that signals the start of an attack

warray to make war upon

washland a plain periodically flooded by a river

wasserman a mythical sea-monster, part-man and thought to destroy ships

waveson goods which appear floating on the sea after a shipwreck **wayment** mourning; lamentation; grief

weald a wood or forest; a wooded land or region; also, an open country **weasand** the windpipe or trachea

weathercock a weathervane; any thing or person that turns easily and frequently; a fickle, inconstant person

weazen thin; sharp; withered; wizened **weftage** texture

wegotism excessive use of the pronoun "we" in speech or writing **wegotist**

weissnichtwo an indefinite, unknown, or imaginary locale [from a novel by Thomas Carlyle and German for know-not-where]

welkin the visible regions of the air; the vault of heaven; the sky; the firmament; the region above the clouds; "When storms the welkin rend." – Wordsworth

weltanschauung a person's or a group's conception, philosophy or view of the world; a worldview [German (world-view)]

welter to tumble about, esp. in anything foul or defiling; to wallow; to rise and fall, as waves; "When we welter in pleasures and idleness, then we eat and drink with drunkards." – Latimer; "The weltering waves." – Milton

wester to move or turn to the west; a strong west wind, esp. a storm-bringing one **westering**

westing a distance west of a datum line on a map or chart; a distance traveled westward

wetwork work that involves killing people

wheeple to whistle ineffectually

whelm to cover; to submerge; to engulf; to bury; to overcome with emotion; to throw (something) over a thing so as to cover it

whitesmith a white iron worker; an iron worker who does finishing work, but not forging

whizbang someone that is explosive in their success, skill or effectiveness

widdendream or **widdrim** a mental state of confusion or extreme excitement; a blind fury; an insane outburst [Scottish from Old English]

widdershins or **withershins** counterclockwise; moving in a counterclockwise, left-handed or contrary direction; unlucky   **widdiful** someone who deserves to be hanged

wifty scatterbrained, ditzy

wildered bewildered; perplexed; "Again the wildered fancy dreams / Of spouting fountains, frozen as they rose" – Bryant

wilding not tame, domesticated, or cultivated; wild; a plant that grows without cultivation

wimple a fold or pleat in cloth; a ripple, as on water; a curve or bend; a flag or streamer

windbound unable to sail because of high winds, or winds blowing toward shore

windjammer a large iron-hulled, square-rigged sailing ship with three or more masts

windlestraw a tall, thin, perhaps feeble person; something flimsy or insubstantial

windthrow the uprooting or felling of trees by the wind

winkle to remove something from a position, esp with force, as by prying; twinkle

winterbourne a stream or spring that flows only in winter or only after rains

winterkill the human, animal or plant mortality resulting from lethal wintry conditions

wisenheimer a wiseguy, a know-it-all; a self-assertive and arrogant person [from wise + German enheimer, found in such surnames as Oppenheimer, Frankenheimer, Schottenheimer] **wist** to know; to be aware of

wistly attentively; earnestly; intently **witeless** blameless

witticaster a witling; someone that tries to be witty, but mostly fails

witzelsucht a tendency to tell inappropriate or pointless stories and jokes; excessive facetiousness

wold a wood; a forest; a plain or low hill; a country without wood, whether hilly or not

wondermonger one who performs, pretends to perform, or promises miracles

wonderwork a wonderful work or act; miracle; thaumaturgy; "Wonderworks of God and Nature's hand." – Byron

wonky lopsided, misaligned; shaky, wobbly, unstable; weak, unreliable **wontless** unaccustomed

woodnote a song or call like that of a forest bird; natural, spontaneous musical note or song; "So you'll live, you'll live, Young Fellow My Lad / In the gleam of the evening star, / In the wood-note wild and the laugh of the child, / In all sweet things that are." – Robert Service

woodreeve the steward of a forested area, esp. in England

workshy disinclined to work; lazy

worksome industrious; laborious; labor-intensive

wowser an annoying and puritan killjoy

wreak to execute in vengeance or passion; to inflict; to express forcefully

writhen having a twisted or distorted form

wuthering to make a rushing or roaring sound, esp. as by wind **wynd** alley; lane

wyrd fate or destiny; fate personified, esp. one of the three Weird Sisters popularized in Shakespeare's Macbeth

wyvern mythical creature resembling a dragon but with only two legs and a barbed tail

Xanadu the summer capital of Kublai Khan's empire; "In Xanadu did Kubla Khan / a stately pleasure-dome decree: / Where Alph, the sacred river, ran/Through caverns measureless to man/Down to a sunless sea" – Coleridge

xanthochromic yellow in color

xanthodontous having yellow teeth

xanthodont a person with yellow teeth

xanthophyll a yellow pigment widely distributed in plants and animals, one noticeable instance of which is the yellowing in autumn leaves; alternate term for lutein

xanthous yellow-brown

xenial hospitable, esp. to visiting strangers or foreigners; friendly; of the relation between host & guest

xenium a present given to a guest or stranger, or to a foreign ambassador; any compulsory gift

xenobombulate to malinger or shirk duties

xenogenesis a foreign origin or source; in biology, the production of an offspring that is unlike either of its parents **xenogenous** caused by something foreign; originating outside an organism

xenoglossy knowledge of a language one never learned in the normal fashion

xenolalia able to speak a language one never studied

xenomania a strong preference for foreign customs, manners, or institutions; the gaining of great pleasure from meeting strangers or visiting foreign countries

xenomorphic having a strange form; in an unusual form

xenophilia an attraction or love of foreign people, manners, or culture

xeric said of a habitat with very little moisture, or of an organism that can live in such an environment

xerophagy a restrictive diet (bread and water, for example) as a punishment or a religious form of discipline

xerothermic dry and hot **xiphoid** like a sword; ensiform; sword-shaped **xylogenous** living on wood

xyloid resembling wood; having the nature of wood; ligneous

xylomancy divination using pieces of burning wood

xylophagous eating wood

yarak in falconry, a super-alert state where the bird is hungry (but not weak) and ready to hunt [Arabic]

yestreen yester-evening; yesternight; last night; last evening

yclept called; cried out; named; past participle of clepe

ylem in alchemy, the material from which the chemical elements developed

ylem in cosmology, the primordial matter of the universe which existed before the Big Bang and the creation of the elements [Latin hylem (matter)]

yoctosecond one septillionth of a second

yokefellow or **yokemate** a partner; a work associate; a mate

yomp a strenuous long-distance march carrying a heavy burden; making such a march

yonderly aloof; psychically distant, esp. in a gloomy fashion

yonic in the shape of a vulva or vagina; female equivalent of phallic

zabernism the misuse or abuse of military authority; bullying

zaffre or **zaffer** a cobalt blue color

zaftig (zoff'-tig) (of a woman) full-bosomed; having a plump and sexually attractive figure; voluptuous, well-proportioned; [Yiddish zaftik (juicy, succulent)]

zappy lively; energetic; entertaining

zarzuela a comic Spanish operetta

zazzy flashy; shiny; stylish

zeitgeber a rhythmically occurring environmental cue, such as a change in light or temperature, that helps regulate the biological clock of an organism

zeitgeist the spirit of the age; the taste, outlook, and spirit characteristic of a particular era

zelatrix older nun who oversees the behavior of younger nuns [Latin female zealot]   **zelophobia** a fear of jealousy

zealotic in the manner of a zealot; zealous; fanatic

zenzizenzizenzic the eighth power of a number

zeptosecond one sextillionth of a second

zibeline sable pelt; a thick woolen fabric with a silky nap

zizz a buzzing sound; a nap   **zoanthropy** a monomania in which one thinks they're an animal

zoetic pertaining to life; alive   **zoonic** pertaining to animals
zounds! an exclamation expressing surprise and wonder
zugzwang in chess, when a player would prefer not to move
    at all, but is forced to make a disadvantageous move
zymurgy the science of fermentation in brewing, distilling,
    wine-making, etc.

Supplemental Words of Beauty or Interest

acropolis adieux aegis afire aeon aerie aesthete affluential
afterpiece after-years ageless aghast air-castle alchemical
alienage amatory ambrosia amorphous amusive
anathematize anomalous apotheosis apparition aqueous
aquiline aquiver arboreous archon ascendant aspirant
astrophile asunder august aural aureate auriferous
aurora polaris aurorean austral avifauna axemaster azan
bachelorship barrowman bechance becloud bedfast
bedwork behoof behowl beleaguered bellygod belvedere
bemad bemazed bemonster benighted bereft besprent
bestial besuited bete noire bethump betwixt bicorporal
bident bilabial biland bitangent blackguard blackwash
blinkered blowzy blueblooded bondmaid bonhomie
boscage breastwork brownshort brumal bucolic bulbacious
bullyrook cachinate cacophonous caper-cutting caperous
capricious carcass-roofing catacomb caterwaul catharsis
celerity celestial celestine centuried chapfallen chasm
Cherubim choleric chrysalis cipher circumambulate
circumboreal circumferentially clandestine clevis
clinkum-clankum clodpated cloud-drift cloud-kissing
cloudland cloudlet cloudscape cloud-woven cloying
coagulum cocksure coextensive colossal complot
conchiferous contradistinction convivial coralloid courtcraft
countercharm counterglow countermarch counterspy
cracksman cragsman craven creedsman crescent crystalline
cumuli cupidity curl-cloud cutlass cyclopic cynosure dacha
dalesman darkling dauntless dayshine deathsman
decadescent demesne demos desacralized descry detritus

diadem dirk disgorge disport dolorous draconian dramshop dreamful dreamingly dreamland dreamlessly dreamscape dreamt dripple drollery dulcet dunnage dynastical ebullient echelon efferent effervescent effluent eiderdown élan vital eldritch elixir eloquence elusory embosom embowered embracive emmarble empress enchant encloud endarkening endpleasure engild engirdle engrail enrapt enrapture envisage epoch erstwhile especial euphony evanesce evenfall eventuate everliving eviternity execrable exfiltrate extrospection eyebeam eyewater eyewink eyrie fadeless fair-faced fairyland fathomless faunal featherly feline felinity femalize femineity feral fetid finespun finiteless flaxen fleeced fleeciness florescent floriated florid floriferous floriform florisitic flowerage footfall footling forechosen foredeep foreland forelock forename forenoon forepleasure foretaste foretime foretoken forgettery forlorn fraught freshet frond frothy fungacious futurity gabbling gambol ghastly glade glitteratti gloaming godling Gordian Knot grandiloquent grotesquerie greensward grief-shot halcyon hegira hellbroth highflown hippogriff hitherto honey-tongued horizonless ilk ill-used illiberal illimitable illstarred illume Illuminati imbue immethodical impalpable imperiousness imponderable incantation incarnate ineffable infinity ingathering ingress inimitable inordinately insensate interlace interlude interminable interpenetrate inviolate iridescent ironhearted irrespective joie de vivre joust junoesque juvenescent juxtapose knell knight-errant labyrinthine lachrymose laconic lactarium lactiferous lamasery lardaceous lea leathern legionary legislatress legislatrix leonine licentious lightsome liliaceous Lilliputian limpid lionize loquacious lotus eater lotusland love charm lovelass lovelorn lovesome lucre luff lupine madding maelstrom maidenhead maidenry malefic mammiferous mammilla manacle manful marginalia mercurial mesmeric miasmic mirrored miserabilist mistbow monomaniacal moribund multipotent murthering mystification mythic nacreousness nadiral naiad nares napery nascent natant nebulochaotic necromantic necropolis necropolitan necrosis nectarous nether nightfall nimbus nirvanic nook-shotten numerable oblivion ocular oddish omnificent omnistrain opacify optionality oracle otherworldly outlander outsweeten overabound overawe overbold overbrow overperch oversoul overstink palaver palliative pallid panache pang pansophy paradigm paradimensional paradisal paragon paramour parapet pariah pasturage pendulous perchance perdurable peregrine knell phallocentric phantasma phantasmagorical phantasmal phantasmata phantasy phial philter piffling pinchpenny piscifauna plethoric plateaux plexus pluvial poriferous porpentine portative portend postbellum postdiluvian prang precipitous preternuptial primacy princekin princeling prismatic protean puerile pulchrify pupatation purse-proud purulent quandary quaver quicksand quicksilver quietus quintessential quisling quixotic quondam raillery rakish rammish rarify ravage razorable redolent refractive refulgent regnal rejuvenescent relume relumine renascent rhapsodic riant rill rime roan rune saccharine sacrosanct sagacious saintstress salient salvific saturnine satyr scansion scintillant seagirt seemings semblance semblative serous sevennight sheeple sibilant sightsome silhouette singular skyborne skyey snail cloud spannew spate specter spellbound spellful spheral spirituous springtide stinkard stratagem stupefacient suavities sub rosa subadolescent subsume suffuse summertree sun-bright sunbeam sunbow sunburst sundart sunder sunglow surprisal suspiration susurration sward syntactic tanling thanatoid thrall threnody throes thunderblast thunderpeal thunderstroke thundrous top gallant torpid torrid tortuose transect transfix translocation translucent transpierce tremulous triflorous trilemma trippingly truepenny tsunamic ubersexual ubiquitous umber underlick undraped undulate unearthly unfledged unfool ungirt unhorse unmindful unmuzzle unparalleling unplumbed unstudied untoward untrammeled unutterable vagary vamphorn vampiric varletry vellum venturesome verboten verdant vernal versecraft versification vertex viatic vicissitudinous vinquish violaceous violescent viperine viperous visage viscera vitreous vividity vivification vixenish voidance volant voluminous voluptuary vulgarian waft weft whence whiffler wile wistful witling wondrous wraithlike wreathe wunderkind yawp zephyrus

THE END

Made in the USA
Columbia, SC
13 June 2022